THE

CULTURAL TRADITIONS
DICTIONARY

GARY LAW

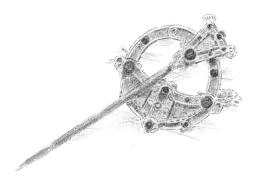

Illustrations by
TONY O'NEILL

THE
BLACKSTAFF
PRESS

BELFAST

First published in 1998 by
The Blackstaff Press Limited
3 Galway Park, Dundonald, Belfast BT16 2AN, Northern Ireland
in association with
the Cultural Diversity Programme of the Community Relations Council

Typeset by Techniset Typesetters, Newton-le-Willows, Merseyside

Printed in Northern Ireland by W. & G. Baird Limited

A CIP catalogue record for this book is available from the British Library

ISBN 0-85640-636-8

Acknowledgements

Thanks are due to a number of people who so willingly gave assistance and advice in the preparation of many entries for this dictionary, particularly Tony Buckley, the Reverend David Cooper, Dr Ian Ellis, Matt Fitzpatrick, Gordon Gillespie, Robbie Hannan, the Reverend William Haslett, John Killen, Cecil Kilpatrick, Gordon Lucy, Aodán Mac Póilin, Seamus McAleenan, Pat McKay, Alvin Mullan, Father Martin O'Callaghan, Lee Reynolds. Apologies to anyone whose name has been inadvertently omitted.

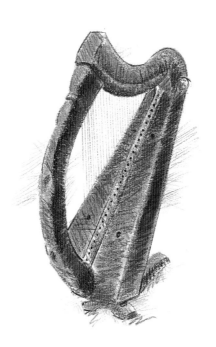

Preface

Cultural traditions is a phrase which has been heard over and over again in Northern Ireland for quite a number of years, but what does it actually mean? A culture can perhaps be considered as an identifiable lifestyle and range of values and attitudes belonging to one group of people which differentiates them from another group. Adding the word tradition seems to underscore the notion that these practices and values have become deeply embedded with the passing of generation after generation.

To encapsulate the broad spectrum of what might be considered 'culture' in Northern Ireland in a dictionary of 227 entries averaging 200 words each means, inevitably, that some things are going to be left out, complex subjects are going to be simplified and topics which might merit whole books to themselves are going to be boiled down to their barest essence. Despite these limitations, the intention of the book is to provide a useful and hopefully enlightening starting point for anyone wishing to explore the rich cultural diversity that exists within Northern Ireland.

The idea for the book originated with the Cultural Diversity Programme of the Community Relations Council. A list of proposed entries was drawn up after a series of consultations between members of the group, the publishers, Blackstaff Press, myself and a variety of knowledgeable people in various fields. The suggested entries were originally arranged under subject headings such as history, sport, music, politics, folklore, religion and symbols. Unsurprisingly, there were far too many of them and the unwieldy number then had to be whittled down to a suitable total. The final tally was originally set at 200 but that barrier was easily broken and a halt had to be called at 227. Even in the very last stages of production there were still difficult decisions to be made over what could be added and what had to be omitted.

It should be noted that in compiling these entries it was not my intention to pass any kind of judgement on the moral worthiness of a particular subject but rather to try to see the topic from the point of view of those for whom it is part of their culture.

In the end, a book such as this can only hope to skim the surface of a culture as complex as ours, but what it might serve to illustrate is that respect and tolerance is enhanced by knowledge of our neighbours' beliefs. A future where everyone agrees is not desirable, but one where differences are respected surely is.

GARY LAW
NEWCASTLE, COUNTY DOWN
SEPTEMBER 1998

THE
CULTURAL TRADITIONS
DICTIONARY

Accordion

The modern accordion, invented in Vienna in 1829, developed from the melodeon, a free-reed bellows instrument which gained in popularity in the nineteenth century when it became a favourite accompanying instrument for set dancing. The melodeon was in turn eclipsed by the button accordion in the early twentieth century and that instrument has now ceded some ground to the piano accordion. However, the button accordion remains a more favoured instrument for ensemble traditional music because it produces less volume than its keyboard cousin and is therefore less likely to drown out other instruments. The button accordion is sometimes used by marching bands because it is less cumbersome than the piano accordion.

See also
Concertina

Act of Union

The United Irishmen's failed rebellion in 1798 and the support, albeit ineffective, that it had received from France convinced the British prime minister, William Pitt, that unifying the Dublin and Westminster parliaments would be the surest way of ending Irish hopes for independence and safeguarding Britain's strategic 'back door'. The chief gatherers of support in Ireland for the passing of the act were Lord Cornwallis, commander in chief of the forces which quelled the 1798 rebellion, and Lord Castlereagh, a Presbyterian landowner in County Down. Both men aimed to include Catholic Emancipation within the Act of Union, and although this was vetoed by the Irish parliament, Pitt promised to pursue the goal after the act was passed. This pledge gained the support of Catholics who had sufficient wealth and property to vote, and in 1800 the Irish parliament passed the Union Bill, effectively voting itself out of existence. The United Kingdom of Great Britain and Ireland came into being on 1 January 1801.

See also Rebellion of 1798, Shamrock, Union Jack, United Irishmen

Ancient Order of Hibernians

Although formed in the USA as late as 1838, Hibernians deliberately use the word 'ancient' in their title to stress a lineage stretching back much further. The organisation claims to be the most recent incarnation of a long line of societies formed to defend Catholic interests in the eighteenth century, such as Ribbonmen and Defenders. Membership of the Ancient Order of Hibernians (AOH) mushroomed in Ireland during the early years of the twentieth century following the appointment of Belfast Nationalist politician, Joe Devlin, to the presidency of its ruling body, the Board of Erin. In the four years up to 1909, the number of members swelled from 10,000 to 60,000, and it continued to rise to around 170,000 by the outbreak of World War I. The Hibernians operated not only as a friendly society, providing welfare insurance for members, but also as a social club

A

and a focus for religious studies and events. The insurance aspect is no longer part of its activities but it continues to act as a religion-based fraternity and social club. Through the order's use of parades, symbols and various rituals and its defence of a religious ethos, it is often regarded as the Catholic counterpart of the Orange Order. AOH members wear collarettes adorned with a range of emblems, carry banners depicting images from Catholicism, nationalism and Celtic heritage at parades, march to the accompaniment of bands, and conclude their processions with speeches and religious ceremonies at a 'field'. The traditional parade day for the AOH is 15 August, the Feast of the Assumption, and some will also take part in Saint Patrick's Day processions.

See also Banner, Defenders, Nationalism, Orange Order, Red Hand, Shamrock

Angelus

A devotional prayer said by members of the Catholic faith at 6 a.m., 12 noon and 6 p.m. The prayer is drawn from the description of the angel Gabriel's Annunciation to the Virgin Mary in Saint Luke's Gospel. The Angelus earns its name from the first two words of the prayer in Latin, *angelus Domini,* 'the angel of the Lord'. It was devised as a means by which the public could join in the devotions of monks at specific times, and a bell would be sounded as a reminder. The Angelus bell is rung in three groups of three strikes, followed by one group of nine strikes.

A

Anglican *see* Church of Ireland

Apprentice Boys of Derry

The Apprentice Boys of Derry is an organisation primarily concerned with commemorating different events associated with the siege of that city in 1689. Its name is derived from the tradition that it was due to the actions of

thirteen apprentice boys in shutting the city's gates that Derry was saved from being overrun by Jacobite forces on the eve of the Williamite Wars. At the heart of the Apprentice Boys organisation are a number of 'parent clubs', each named after personalities associated with the siege. Each parent club has many branches, which are amalgamated into groups (for example, the County Down Amalgamated Clubs) that roughly correspond to districts in the Orange Order structure. Members of the Apprentice Boys of Derry need not necessarily be Orangemen, but all members must be initiated within Derry's walls, on ceremonies usually carried out on either 18 December (the date on which the apprentice boys shut the gates) or 12 August (the day the siege ended). The Apprentice Boys' collarettes are coloured crimson to symbolise the defiant 'bloody flag' that was raised over Derry during the siege.

See also Orange Order, Sash, Siege of Derry

A

Arch

A traditional feature of the Twelfth of July celebrations, early arches were often decorated with flowers. Today they tend to be adorned with Orange, Black and Arch Purple symbols added at the discretion of the builders. In the past rival neighbourhoods would vie with each other to create the most impressive arch, even though the structure might not be situated on the marching route. Arches are most commonly placed today outside the local Orange hall, along the route of the main district Twelfth procession, and at the entrance to the 'field' at the end of the parade.

See also Orange Lily, Orange Order, Royal Arch Purple, Royal Black Institution, Twelfth of July

A

B Specials

The largest contingent of the Ulster Special Constabulary, a force formed in 1920 to supplement the Royal Irish Constabulary, which was stretched to its limit during the military campaign for Irish independence. The Ulster Special Constabulary was divided into three sections: the A Specials were a full-time force of around two thousand men; the B Specials consisted of almost twenty thousand part-timers; and the C Specials were a reserve force of unspecified numbers who were only to be called upon in cases of extreme emergency. Following partition and the formation of the Royal Ulster Constabulary, the B Specials remained active during a period of continuing violence which accompanied the birth of the northern state. A number of B Specials were killed in IRA attacks and members of the force also took part in reprisal actions, many of which were of a sectarian nature. The B Specials continued to be mobilised during periods of increased violence for the next forty years. One of the first violent deaths of the Troubles which began in 1969 is attributed to the B Specials after they fired into a crowd at a civil rights demonstration in Armagh. Two months later, the disbandment of the Ulster Special Constabulary was proposed and duly enacted.

See also Civil Rights Movement, Partition

Bagpipes

The bagpipes have existed in various forms throughout Europe and Asia for at least three thousand years. The first evidence of the instrument being used in Ireland dates back to the eleventh century although it is certain the pipes were played here long before that. The piper was part of the military establishment in Ireland by the early seventeenth century

B

and the music of the bagpipes could also be heard at funerals and sporting occasions around this time. The best-known version of the instrument is the Scottish highland pipes, which are sounded when the player inflates the bag through a blowpipe and the air is forced out through the chanter, on which the melody is played, and the drones. By fingering the holes on the chanter, the piper produces the different notes. The Scottish lowland pipes are based on similar principles except that the bag is inflated with a bellows rather than a mouthpiece.

See also Royal Scottish Pipe Band Association, Uilleann Pipes

Banner

The use of banners during processions in Ireland is a long-standing and widespread tradition. Most commonly associated with the loyal orders, banners have also been used for many years by a variety of trade unions, guilds, societies and brotherhoods. In the Orange tradition, lodges originally walked behind flags at demonstrations, but these were quickly replaced by the more popular banner at the beginning of the nineteenth century. Most Orange banners depict scenes from the Williamite Wars while those of the Royal Black Institution usually employ imagery from the Bible. One of the most notable suppliers of Orange banners over the years has been the English trade union banner-makers, Tutill's, whose founder developed a process which enabled the painting of images

B

directly onto silk banners, thus ending the need for difficult-to-produce embroidered banners. The Belfast firm of Bridgett's also supplied a large proportion of Orange banners in the North for more than one hundred years. Other societies to employ banners in their processions include the Irish National Foresters, which at one time was the biggest friendly society in Ireland, and the Ancient Order of Hibernians, whose banners often include the figure of Saint Patrick as their central motif.

See also Ancient Order of Hibernians, Irish National Foresters, Orange Order, Royal Black Institution, Twelfth of July

Banns

A quasi-legal pre-marriage ritual within the Church of Ireland. If the couple to be married are both members of the Church of Ireland, the banns may be read on consecutive Sundays for three weeks before the wedding ceremony as an optional alternative to marriage by licence. The reading of the banns announces the forthcoming marriage to the wider church community and also invites anyone with objections to the union to voice them. The tradition derives from the period when the Church of Ireland was the Established Church in Ireland and has since largely gone out of fashion.

See also Church of Ireland

Banshee

An apparition whose manifestation is said to be an omen of the impending death of someone close to the person who sees it. The banshee, whose name is derived from the Irish phrase *bean sí,* meaning 'fairy woman', is usually depicted as an old woman, often seen combing her long hair, and her appearance is accompanied by loud wails of grief. One of the best-

B

known banshees was Aibhill, whose apparition was seen by Brian Boru on the night before the Battle of Clontarf in 1014. On the following day Brian was killed during the fighting.

Baptist Church

Although relatively small in Northern Ireland, the Baptist church is one of the largest Protestant communions in the world, with over 42 million members, the vast majority of whom live in the USA. According to the 1991 census, there are 19,500 Baptists in Northern Ireland, making it the fifth largest denomination. The modern Baptist church traces its roots back to the teachings of John Smyth, who in 1609 championed the idea of the baptism of committed Christians as the foundation for a church. Baptisms are carried out by immersing the candidate in water and only those old enough to understand and accept the responsibilities of Christian faith are baptised. Particular Baptists were founded in 1633 by Calvinists who believed that salvation will only be granted to a select devout few, while Strict Baptists restrict Holy Communion solely to baptised believers. However, the mainstream Baptist church has adopted a policy of open communion in which all Christian believers are welcomed to their services of Holy Communion. The Baptist church was introduced to Ireland by chaplains and officers who came from England with Oliver Cromwell's army in the mid-seventeenth century. Many of the churches they founded were Particular Baptist institutions, although there were also mainstream Baptist churches. The Baptist Union of Great Britain and Ireland came into being following the formation of the Baptist Union in England in 1813 and later the Baptist Union of Ireland was formed. Although Baptist churches share a fellowship of belief, there is no central authority and each church is autonomous.

Barony

Baronies were originally defined as areas ruled by chieftains who pledged their allegiance to the English crown. The gradual adoption of this English feudal

B

system of land division began in medieval times in Ireland, although it was not until the plantation years of the early seventeenth century that it became fully effective in Ulster. Later the boundaries of the baronies were redrawn so that they would fit in more neatly with the county divisions. As with other land divisions, the size of baronies varies widely, and some were divided into sections, usually known as lower, middle and upper.

See also County, Parish, Townland

Battle of the Boyne

A decisive battle in the power struggle for the English throne at the end of the seventeenth century. It was precipitated by the deposal of Catholic James II by Protestant William III (William of Orange) in the Glorious Revolution of 1688–9. James's daughter Mary was married to William. Supporters of James's claim to the throne (called Jacobites, from the Latin version of James, *Jacobus*) actively pursued his restoration in Ireland and Scotland. When William landed in Carrickfergus in June 1690 with a force comprising half a dozen different nationalities, the scene was set for a contest that would decide the issue in Ireland at least. The two opposing forces met on the banks of the River Boyne, west of Drogheda, on 1 July 1690. The superior firepower and numbers of the Williamite forces won the day, but the victory was far from overwhelming. The Jacobite army escaped almost intact and continued to fight a rearguard action for a further year. However, James's hope of using Ireland as a platform for regaining the English throne had been effectively ended. He fled to France and William captured Dublin. Ulster Protestants viewed the outcome of the battle as a victory for their beliefs and a safeguard for the plantation in the wake of the 1641 rebellion. The modern commemoration of the Battle of the Boyne takes place on 12 July because of the change from the Julian calendar to the Gregorian calendar adopted in England in 1752. In fact, the Battle of Aughrim, a far more bloody campaign than the Boyne, was the only conflict of the Williamite Wars to take place on 12 July.

See also Huguenots, Plantation, Rebellion of 1641, Sham Fight, Siege of Derry, Twelfth of July

Battle of the Diamond

A brief affray between the Catholic Defenders and a Protestant faction (which may have been the Orange Boys, founded in 1793, or the Peep o' Day Boys, or a mixture of both) which led to the subsequent formation of the Orange Order in September 1795. The Diamond is a small hamlet at a crossroads about two miles from Loughgall, County Armagh.

The two opposing forces gathered here after several years of bitter sectarian violence in the county. Despite efforts to calm the situation, the battle began when the Defenders attacked and burnt Dan Winter's spirit grocers in the centre of the hamlet. Those inside resisted but were eventually forced to flee up a nearby hill where the Protestant faction was based. The Defenders followed, but were cut down by successive volleys of gunfire. Around thirty or forty of them were killed and a further fifty wounded. The whole battle probably lasted no more than fifteen minutes, and when it was all

B

over, tradition has it that the victors met in a field near Dan Winter's house to form the Orange Order and the first Orangeman was initiated beside a spring well in Dan's garden.

See also Defenders, Orange Order, Peep o' Day Boys

Battle of the Somme

One of the major battles of World War I in which half the men of the 36th (Ulster) Division – around 5,500 – were killed or wounded within the first two days of fighting. The event has assumed major significance within Protestant and loyalist symbolism because the battle began on 1 July, the old calendar date of the Battle of the Boyne, and the scale of the sacrifice was seen as emblematic of Ulster's loyalty to Britain. Four posthumous Victoria Crosses were won by men of the Ulster Division. Although formed largely from the Ulster Volunteer Force, which had been established in the pre-war years to resist Irish home rule, the Ulster Division was not a 100 per cent Protestant detachment, nor were its ranks exclusively drawn from Ulster. Also involved in the long Somme campaign were soldiers of the 16th (Irish) Division, whose members were drawn mostly from the pro-home-rule National Volunteers. This detachment suffered almost as much as the Ulster Division, with 4,300 men killed or wounded between 3 September and 9 September 1916.

See also Titanic, Young Citizen Volunteers

Bawn

A defensive courtyard attached to manor houses built during the plantation of Ulster in the seventeenth century. Each new landlord granted ownership of

B

one thousand acres or more was expected to build a bawn, which did not enclose the manor house but was more often two or three high walls adjoining the house to create a defendable courtyard. Derived from the Irish *bábhún,* the word bawn often became part of the name of a town or village, such as Hamiltonsbawn, County Armagh.

See also Plantation

Bealtaine

One of the significant dates in the Celtic calendar, *Bealtaine* was a festival held on the first day of May, celebrating the end of the winter and the onset of spring and summer. A symbolic bonfire was one of the central features of the celebrations. *Bealtaine* is the Irish language word for the month of May.

See also Celts, Lughnasa, Samhain

Belfast Blitz

When 180 German bombers attacked the poorly defended city of Belfast on the night of Easter Tuesday, 15 April 1941, the carnage that resulted was the worst suffered by any city in the British Isles, outside London, in a single air raid during World War II. The huge death toll – at least nine hundred people died – was caused by bombs that landed in dense housing areas north and east of the city centre. The civil defence authorities and emergency services were ill-prepared for the scale of the attack, co-ordination and discipline broke down, and hundreds of fires started by incendiary devices raged out of control. An urgent telegram seeking help was sent to the *taoiseach,* Eamon de Valera, and he immediately agreed to send fire engines from Dublin, Drogheda, Dundalk and Dún Laoghaire to Belfast, effectively violating Ireland's wartime neutrality. In the end, most of the fires burnt themselves out. Whole families had perished, people who fled to air raid shelters had been killed when the shelters were hit by bombs, many bodies were never even found, and others remained unidentified. A memorial with the simple inscription, 'Sacred to the memory of unidentified victims of enemy action, Belfast, April

B

1941', was later erected in Milltown Cemetery. A second attack came on the night of 4–5 May 1941, and this time the targets were the harbour, the aircraft factory and the shipyards. After the raids some one hundred thousand Belfast people fled to the countryside.

Bishop *see* Cathedral

Black Pig's Dyke

Part of a series of intermittent earthworks that appear to form a defensive wall stretching from the border of counties Down and Armagh to the Donegal coast. Constructed some one hundred years before the birth of Christ, it separates the province of Ulster from the rest of Ireland. These defensive barriers are believed to have guarded the natural invasion routes into Ulster between loughs, bogs and mountains and the various sections are known by different names (such as the Dorsey, from *doirse*, meaning 'doors' or 'gates', in south Armagh). The section known as the Black Pig's Dyke, in counties Armagh and Monaghan, is believed to have taken its name from the myth that the earthworks were torn up from the ground by the tusks of a magical black boar.

Bodhrán

A small hand-held drum in which the skin is stretched over a circular frame and beaten with a double-headed wooden stick. The *bodhrán* was used not only as a drum but also as a farming and domestic implement as far back as pre-Christian times. In the fields it was used to separate chaff from the grain and in the home it doubled as a container for storing and serving food. Initially, the home-made *bodhrán* was created by bending a

B

pliable branch into a circle and stretching the skin over it, whereas nowadays the professionally made *bodhrán* frame is constructed from layers of plywood. The skin used for the drum is traditionally goatskin, although skins of other animals are also used. Over the years the typical size of a *bodhrán* has become smaller, to reduce the drum's volume for accompanying instruments such as fiddles, flutes and uilleann pipes, and the sticks used to beat it have become lighter to allow for more intricate ornamentation during playing.

Bog

Large areas of bogland (from the Irish *bogach*, meaning 'soft ground') developed in Ireland in the period following the last ice age. They were situated in areas where water could not easily drain from the land, and in the sixteenth century it was estimated that one-quarter of the island was covered by bogland. During the plantation, many native Irish families were driven from their lands and were forced to live in the wetlands (hence the disparaging term 'bog-Irish'). Bogs have been put to a variety of uses over the centuries. They were often used as storage places for butter, and some samples of bog-butter are still occasionally uncovered during turf-cutting. Bodies were sometimes disposed of in bogs, and several well-preserved corpses have been discovered. Turf dug from the bog has been used as a fuel in Ireland throughout recorded history. Traditionally, it was cut by hand using a spade known as a *sleán*, which had a right-angled edge to the blade to enable a sod to be cut with a single stroke. Around 90 per cent of bogland in Ireland has been lost through drainage or overworking and many of the remaining areas are now the subject of conservation efforts.

See also Plantation

Book of Armagh

The earliest surviving written text in Ireland, the Book of Armagh dates back to AD 807. A religious work written in Latin, its pages contain the New

B

15

Testament, Saint Patrick's Confession, two biographies of Patrick and one of Saint Martin of Tours, and an essay arguing the case for Armagh as the ecclesiastical capital of Ireland. This last claim received the backing of Brian Boru during his attempt to conquer Ulster in 1005. In return for his support, Brian ordered that a passage be added to the book describing him as *Imperator Scottorum* – Emperor of the Irish.

See also Saint Patrick

Booley

A traditional farming practice involving the movement of sheep and cattle from lowland winter feeding grounds to higher summer pastures in surrounding hills and mountains. Often the animals would be accompanied by their owners, who would spend the summer in temporary huts and dwellings in the hills.

Born Again

A colloquial term used to describe a positive personal awareness of Christian conversion, renewal and salvation. Being born again is an experience usually associated with Protestantism, which places strong emphasis on an individual's personal relationship with God, and may often be the result of contact with evangelistic outreach and inspirational preaching. People who have been born again will often describe themselves as 'saved' and will be able to recall the exact time and circumstances of their rebirth in the hope that it will prove an inspiration to others.

See also Evangelism, Protestantism

B

Boundary Commission

The proposal to set up a boundary commission to review the dividing line between North and South in Ireland was contained in the Anglo-Irish Treaty, signed by representatives of Dáil Éireann and the British government in December 1921. The treaty provided for the creation of the twenty-six-county Irish Free State, but fell short of granting full independence to Ireland, causing deep divisions which led to civil war. The proposal for a boundary commission within the treaty led southern nationalists to hope that more land would be removed from the North to join the South, while unionists living in border areas feared they and their lands were to be handed over to the Free State. The commission's deliberations were postponed for several years because of the Irish Civil War and when it finally did meet in 1924 and 1925, its proposals were considered so insignificant that the existing border which ran along county lines was retained.

See also Free State, Partition

Bowler Hat

The bowler hat, along with a pair of white gloves, is part of the traditional attire of members of the Orange Order and Black preceptories at their annual demonstrations. The origin of the custom of wearing these items is unclear, but it is generally thought that both were a sign of the respectability of the wearer. Some have suggested that since a bowler was often worn by a foreman on building sites or at the shipyard, the hat was a sign of authority. Within some lodges, it is almost an unspoken rule that members parade in bowler hat and gloves – not to do so would be frowned upon – but in most cases to wear or not to wear is a matter of individual taste.

See also Twelfth of July.

B

Boycott

In 1880, when Lord Erne's Mayo tenants socially ostracised the estate manager, Captain Charles Boycott, and refused to deal with him commercially, a new word entered the English language. The boycott, carried out in protest against evictions, proved such a success that the captain was unable to continue in his position and was forced to leave Ireland. The tactic was also used against others who evicted tenants in the years that followed and has continued to be used sporadically ever since, perhaps most notably during the years following partition in 1921 when the South boycotted northern exports – the 'Belfast boycott'.

See also Partition

Boys' Brigade

A youth movement founded in Glasgow in 1883 by William A. Smith, who combined his knowledge of soldiery and Sunday school teaching to create an organisation which would instil discipline in inner-city children and provide a programme of physical activities and Bible study. The Boys' Brigade became established in Ireland with the formation of the First Belfast Company in 1888 and by 1893 there were some twenty-eight companies in the North and a further twenty-one companies in Dublin, most of them connected with the Church of Ireland. Today, around two-thirds of the 353 companies in Northern Ireland are associated with the Presbyterian Church, with others linked to a variety of Protestant churches. A similar organisation for girls, the Girls' Brigade, was founded in 1893. The programme for both organisations continues to focus on physical recreation with a strong religious emphasis.

See also Scout Movement, Sunday School

Brethren

Although Brethren are more widely known around the world as Plymouth Brethren, because the body was supposed to have been founded in Plymouth in 1830, it actually originated in Ireland a few years before that date, and as a result members are known here simply as Brethren. Their house of worship is usually referred to as a gospel hall rather than a church and the congregation is its own self-governing unit. There is no organised ministry within the Brethren and no formalised structure for meetings, although special emphasis is placed upon the breaking of bread each Sunday. Brethren live by strict moral principles which not only govern their personal conduct but also extend to the type of employment they may undertake. In 1849, disputes within the church led to a split into Open Brethren and Exclusive Brethren and there are also several divisions within these groupings. The majority of Brethren are to be found in Western Europe and the USA, although a considerable number are involved in missionary work in the Far East. In 1991 there were 12,500 Brethren in Northern Ireland, making it the sixth largest denomination.

Burning Bush

The symbol of the Presbyterian church was inspired by the biblical story of Moses' encounter with a bush which was on fire but was not consumed, and its use is intended to signify the suffering and endurance of the church. The burning bush was first used as a symbol by French Huguenots in the late sixteenth century, and a century later it began to appear on official documents of the Church of Scotland. The symbol is accompanied by the motto *ardens sed virens*, 'burning but living'. The words are believed to have been coined by the Reverend William Gibson, minister of Rosemary Street Presbyterian church in Belfast, around the year 1842. In Scotland, the motto attached to the symbol is *nec tamen consumebatur*, 'not yet destroyed'.

See also Huguenots, Presbyterian Church

Camogie

The women's version of hurling has been an organised sport with its own standardised rules since 1904. The game derives its name from the Irish language name for a hurling stick, *camán*, and in the early days it generally thrived in urban areas, where it was played mostly by women of independent means and university graduates. In Ulster, for example, camogie was popular amongst women in the urban surroundings of Newry and Belfast during the early years of the century. Given the relatively subordinate status of women in Ireland at that time, it is not surprising that camogie was initially slow to develop; it was almost thirty years before the first all-Ireland competition was held. Today, there are over 150 camogie clubs in Ulster and the game's most successful Ulster county is Antrim, which has won six all-Ireland senior titles. While the sport has close links with the Gaelic Athletic Association, camogie's governing body is completely separate from the GAA. Camogie has its own county boards and provincial councils, and its supreme body is the *ardchomhairle* ('supreme council') which annually elects a president and office bearers as well as adjudicating on all aspects of the game. On the pitch there are relatively few differences between camogie and hurling. Players of both games use a similar-sized *camán* and the rules are roughly the same. However, at the moment there are only twelve players in a camogie team (as opposed to fifteen-a-side in hurling) and the game is played on a reduced-size pitch, but this is set to change from 1999 when camogie teams will adopt the hurling standards of pitch and team size for competitions which run to all-Ireland level.

See also Gaelic Athletic Association, Hurling

Catechism

A handbook used by a broad cross-section of denominations to explain a church's particular doctrine, usually by means of questions and answers. Derived from a Greek word meaning 'to make hear', the term catechism originally applied to the oral teachings given to children and adults before baptism, but by the sixteenth century it had come to refer more

C

usually to the written word. The Anglican catechism in the Book of Common Prayer provides instruction for candidates for confirmation, the Presbyterian catechism focuses on the Westminster Confession, and the Catholic catechism is a four-section manual which not only explains the church's teaching but also addresses contemporary ethical questions.

See also Confirmation, Presbyterian Church

Cathedral

The cathedral is the mother church in a Catholic or Church of Ireland diocese and is the seat of a bishop. The bishop is the central figure of authority and unity within the diocese, and it is the Greek word for bishop, *episcopus* (literally 'overseer') which gives rise to the description of the Catholic Church and the Church of Ireland as episcopal institutions. Both churches have a cathedral chapter which is made up of canons, selected senior clergy from parishes within the diocese. In the Church of Ireland, one of the canons is appointed to the post of archdeacon to assist the bishop in administrative matters, while responsibility for the running of the cathedral is in the hands of the dean. Within the Catholic church, the bishop may be assisted by an auxiliary bishop, plus one or two vicars general, who are responsible for administration, and several vicars forane, who liaise between parishes within the diocese.

See also Catholic Church, Church of Ireland, Synod

C

Catholic

In its widest sense, the term 'Catholic' can be applied to the entire body of Christians of whatever denomination since it means simply 'universal' or 'all-embracing'. This term was first used to describe the early Christian church, which was effectively a single body until it split into the Eastern Orthodox churches and the Western or Latin churches. After this time, the term Catholic became generally associated with the Western churches, and following the Reformation of the sixteenth century it was commonly used to refer to that part of the Western church in communion with Rome. In Ireland, as elsewhere, the term Catholic has become shorthand for Roman Catholic, although it is also used by some Protestant churches to describe their membership of the worldwide Christian faith. The Nicene Creed, a statement of belief shared by Catholics and a number of Protestant denominations, refers to the 'one, holy, catholic and apostolic church'.

See also Catholic Church,
Church of Ireland,
Protestantism

Catholic Church

Both Catholics and Anglicans in Ireland share the belief that the establishment of their respective churches in this country began with the mission of Saint Patrick in the fifth century AD. Their paths diverge at the time of the Reformation when Protestant converts rejected the authority of Rome. With the establishment of the Church of Ireland as the official state church in Ireland, Catholics were severely penalised for their beliefs. In the early seventeenth century Catholics could be fined for not attending an Anglican church. During Cromwell's subjugation of Ireland, priests were forced to flee or else go into hiding, and their congregations had to worship in secret at remote 'Mass rocks'. In 1681 the Catholic primate of all-Ireland, Oliver Plunkett, was executed by Protestant zealots in England. (He was canonised in 1975 and became the first new Irish saint for nearly seven hundred years.) Following the Williamite Wars, the penal laws were introduced in 1695, prohibiting Catholics from voting, holding public office and sitting in parliament. Catholics were also effectively barred from owning any substantial amount of land. Most of these restrictions were repealed in the late eighteenth century, although civil and political rights were not restored until Catholic Emancipation was granted in 1829 following the efforts of Daniel O'Connell's Catholic Association. In the middle of the nineteenth century there was a concerted Catholic religious revival which introduced many European spiritual practices to Ireland and this was followed a century later by the liberalising reforms of the Second Vatican Council. Catholicism remains the largest single denomination in Northern Ireland (605,000 members in 1991) and one of the most notable features of the church is the high level of attendance, particularly in rural areas. Parishes, under the supervision of a parish priest, are grouped into dioceses, each of which is administered by a bishop, and these in turn are grouped into four ecclesiastical provinces – Armagh, Dublin, Cashel and Tuam – which are spiritually led by an archbishop. The archbishop of Armagh is also the primate of all-Ireland, the supreme authority within the Catholic church in Ireland. This position is conferred upon a candidate by Rome, following consultations with clergy and lay people by the Papal Nuncio, the Pope's ambassador.

See also Angelus, Catechism, Cathedral, Catholicism, Chapel, Christian Brothers, Church of Ireland, Confirmation, Corpus Christi, Curate, First Communion, Hail Mary, Holy Communion, Holy Water, Knights of Saint Columbanus, Mass, Missal, Novena, Pioneer Total Abstinence Association, Presbytery, Priest, Retreat, Rosary, Sacred Heart of Jesus, Saint Vincent de Paul, Shrine, Stations of the Cross, Tabernacle, Unction

Cattle Raid of Cooley

The most famous story of the Ulster Cycle of Tales, in Irish the *Táin Bó Cuailnge*, which tells how Queen Medbh of Connacht, jealous of the impressive white bull owned by her husband, snatched the prized Brown Bull of Cooley during a raid on Ulster. The defending warriors were unable to prevent the abduction because they had been rendered helpless by a spell inflicted by Macha, a demi-goddess after whom Emain Macha (Navan Fort) is named. Only the youthful Cú Chulainn was impervious to the debilitating spell and he waged a long single-handed defence, using superhuman warrior skills and magical weapons, to beat overwhelming numbers before the other Ulster warriors overcame Macha's spell and rallied to his aid. Among those Cú Chulainn was forced to fight was his boyhood friend, Ferdia, who was goaded by Queen Medbh into challenging Ulster's mightiest warrior. The battle between the pair lasted for days as neither friend wanted to harm the other, but eventually Cú Chulainn struck a fatal blow, and it was said that his laments at being forced to kill one of his closest friends could be heard as far away as Scotland.

See also Cú Chulainn, Navan Fort, Ulster Cycle of Tales

Céilí

Traditionally, a *céilí* need not involve music or dancing at all but can simply mean a gathering of friends and neighbours in a local house for conversation and 'crack'. Gradually, however, the word *céilí* began to be applied to organised dances in an attempt to stress that they were also social occasions. The first *céilí* organised by the Gaelic League took place in 1897, not in Ireland, but in London, where the entertainment consisted of music and song, step dancing, set dances and waltzes danced to Irish airs.

See also Crack, Gaelic League

C

Celts

Celtic culture came to Ireland some time around 500 BC, sweeping westward across Europe from the eastern part of the Continent and absorbing Britain in the process. The Celts did not establish a nation in Ireland, and indeed may not have been very numerous here, but rather they brought with them a forceful design for living which, over the centuries, assimilated Ireland's pre-Celtic tribes and established a political, legal and social system that influenced the development of the country for almost two thousand years. While the Roman Empire ended Celtic dominance in Britain, the Celts of Ireland retained their culture and adapted it to meet the requirements of Christianity following Patrick's arrival in the fifth century. Writing came to Ireland in the wake of Christianity, and many of the orally handed-down tales of the Celts were recorded for the first time. The Ulster Cycle of Tales, on which much of our assumptions about life in early Celtic times are based, told of the epic Cattle Raid of Cooley, the *Táin Bó Cuailnge*, and of the feats of the warrior, Cú Chulainn. The Celts brought with them the early Irish language, and many of the placenames and family names throughout Ireland are an enduring indicator of their legacy. The distinctive artwork of the Celts is found not only in Ireland but throughout the British Isles and Europe (although the spiral designs often associated with them were in existence in Ireland long before the Celts appeared). Neither the Vikings nor the Normans made such a lasting overall impression on the culture of Ireland, and it was not until the years of the plantation in the early seventeenth century that the Celtic structure of society began to be overwhelmed by the dominance of England.

See also Bealtaine, Cattle Raid of Cooley, Children of Lir, Cruthin, Cú Chulainn, Deirdre of the Sorrows, Flight of the Earls, Irish Language, Lughnasa, Placenames, Samhain, Tuatha Dé Danaan, Ulster Cycle of Tales

25

Champ

A popular food in all parts of Ireland which makes good use of the island's most popular vegetable. Champ is a simple dish consisting of boiled potatoes mixed with milk, butter and scallions, although leeks and even nettles are sometimes used as substitutes. Champ is also a popular dish in Scotland, where the word appears to have originated (meaning 'to mash'). It may also be known in Scotland as thump or stelk. A variation on the dish, red champ, can be made by combining cooked beetroot with potatoes.

See also Potato

Chapel

A place of Christian worship usually associated in Ireland with the Catholic faith, although in England it has a much broader connotation and may be associated with many denominations. In some cases the use of the word 'chapel' may be taken to refer to a non-public place of worship, such as a private church or a house of worship linked to a university or college. The name comes from the Latin word *capella*, meaning 'cape', because the church in which Saint Martin of Tours's sacred cloak was kept came to be called the 'capella church', and the phrase spread into general usage.

Children of Lir

One of the most poignant stories from Celtic mythology, the story of the children of Lir begins with the death of the wife of Lir, a chieftain of the mythical Tuatha Dé Danaan, in childbirth. Left with four children to bring up, Lir married his wife's sister Aoife, but as time progressed Aoife became jealous of the children because she had not borne any of her own. On a trip to a lake in Westmeath, Aoife ordered her servants to kill the children and to say that they had drowned. When the servants refused to carry out her orders, Aoife summoned up a magical spell that turned the children into swans and exiled them to

nine hundred years of
wandering. One of the side
effects of the spell was
that the swans became
beautiful singers, and
when the children returned
to their father his sadness at their
plight was lifted by their inspirational
singing, and he told them to pass on
their gift to the people of Dé Danaan so
that they would become the most famous
singers in the world. As the nine hundred years
of wandering neared an end, the swans went to live
with a Christian hermit in Mayo. One day he was visited by a king
who commanded him to let the swans go as the king wanted them
to sing at a banquet hosted by his new wife. The hermit refused, but
the king snatched the swans and took them to the queen. When
they arrived, however, the swans became human again, taking on the
appearance of very old, white-haired people, and before they died
the hermit baptised them into the Christian faith.

See also Celts, Tuatha Dé
Danaan

Chinese

The largest single immigrant
grouping in Northern Ireland, totalling perhaps eight thousand
people or more, is Chinese. Most of them came here from the rural
area around Hong Kong in the decades after World War II and a
large proportion are employed in the restaurant business, with the
result that there is scarcely a town in the North without at least one
and perhaps as many as five or six Chinese restaurants. The vast
majority of Chinese immigrants live in the Greater Belfast area and
surrounding countryside, with a significant community located in
south Belfast. Most older Chinese people observe beliefs such as
Buddhism or Confucianism, although there is little opportunity for
them to practise their religions locally in appropriate places of

C

worship. A few attend Christian churches and there is also a Chinese Christian church in Belfast. For many Chinese in Northern Ireland, however, the language barrier isolates them from society, although efforts are being made by community groups to overcome this and other problems. In a novel move in 1996, the Progressive Unionist Party, canvassing in south Belfast, produced election literature in Mandarin and Cantonese.

Christian Brothers

A Catholic religious order which owes its foundation to Edmund Ignatius Rice, a charismatic Waterford businessman who turned his back on commerce to set up a school for the education of the poor in the early part of the nineteenth century. In the years that followed the order expanded to meet a need for schools throughout Ireland to educate disadvantaged Catholics and in 1822 the network was formally organised as the Irish Christian Brothers with Rice, now known as Brother Ignatius, as its superior-general. The first Christian Brothers school in England opened three years later, and gradually the organisation spread throughout the world, with schools being set up as far away as Borneo.

Church of Ireland

The Church of Ireland, like the Catholic church in Ireland, claims a descent from the introduction of Christianity to Ireland through the mission of Saint Patrick in the fifth century AD; the lineage of archbishops of Armagh drawn up by the church lists the present incumbent as a direct successor to Patrick. This is central to the church's perception of itself as a uniquely Irish institution. Many Church of Ireland churches are situated on ecclesiastical sites and Armagh cathedral is built upon the site of Patrick's church. A Protestant reformed church, the Church of Ireland nonetheless has many similarities to the Catholic church (both churches share the same one-thousand-year lineage from the arrival of Patrick up to the Reformation in the sixteenth century). Church of Ireland members are also

C

Anglicans, and have full communion with the see of Canterbury, although the archbishop of Canterbury has no jurisdiction over Irish Anglicans. The Church of Ireland has the same basic structures of administration as the Church of England, but unlike that church, the Irish Anglican church was disestablished in 1871 and has no constitutional role. The smallest geographical unit of the Church of Ireland is the parish, and a number of parishes make up a diocese, of which there are twelve in Ireland. The mother church of each diocese is the cathedral, which is the seat of a bishop, a key figure of unity within the church family. The supreme authority in the Church of Ireland is the General Synod under the presidency of the archbishop of Armagh, who is elected by the House of Bishops, a gathering of all twelve bishops in Ireland. The partition of Ireland in 1921 posed particular challenges for the Church of Ireland, with the result that the standard form of morning and evening prayer in Northern Ireland asks God 'to save the Queen', while in the Republic of Ireland the same prayer urges God 'to save the President'. According to the 1991 census, there are 279,000 members of the Church of Ireland living in Northern Ireland, making it the third largest denomination.

See also Banns, Cathedral, Catholic Church, Confirmation, Curate, Holy Communion, Partition, Priest, Protestantism, Rector, Saint Patrick, Select Vestry, Synod

Circuit

A term used within the Methodist church to describe a number of churches grouped together for mutual support. There are 125 Methodist circuits in Ireland, and although some of them may contain only one church, most circuits contain several churches. Representatives of the circuits will serve on District Synods and attend the Annual Conference. The principle of circuits is derived from the Wesleyan idea of sending teams of preachers into particular geographical areas to spread the gospel through a co-operative effort.

See also Methodist Church, Methodist Conference, Synod

Civil Rights Movement

The Northern Ireland Civil Rights Association (NICRA) was formed in early 1967 to campaign for electoral reform, an end to discrimination in employment and public housing allocation, the repeal of the Special Powers Act and the disbanding of the B Specials. The focus of its campaign was the city of Derry where the movement garnered support from a number of local pressure groups as well as from the left-wing students' group, the People's Democracy, which was formed in Belfast in October 1968. Violence flared at a number of protest marches in 1968 and 1969 when the Royal Ulster Constabulary (RUC) banned certain events or loyalists held counter-demonstrations. But it was a loyalist attack on a People's Democracy march from Belfast to Derry at Burntollet Bridge in January 1969 that provided the spark for sustained street violence which led ultimately to an era of widespread bombings and shootings. In the wake of the civil rights campaign, universal

suffrage ('one man, one vote') was introduced in 1969, the
B Specials were disbanded in 1970, the Housing Executive was set
up in 1971, the Fair Employment Agency (later the Fair
Employment Commission) was established in 1976, and the offices
of the Northern Ireland Ombudsman and Commissioner for
Complaints was also created.

See also B Specials,
Gerrymander

Claddagh Ring

A distinctive ring, often used
as a wedding ring, which takes its name from the ancient Galway
village of Claddagh, which is now part of Galway city. Said to have
been created in the sixteenth century, the Claddagh ring is made
from either gold or silver and depicts two hands
holding a heart surmounted by a crown. The
motto 'let love and friendship reign' is often
associated with the ring. Tradition dictates
that if the Claddagh ring is received from a
loved one, it is worn with the heart symbol
pointing towards the wearer's heart, but if that
love and friendship should diminish or disappear
the ring should be worn with the heart facing outwards.

Collarette *see* Sash

Comhaltas Ceoltóirí Éireann

Founded in 1951, Comhaltas
Ceoltóirí Éireann is a thirty-two-county organisation aimed at
promoting excellence in Irish music. CCÉ holds regular classes in a
wide range of instruments and singing, and organises the annual
county, provincial and all-Ireland *fleadhanna*. The organisation also
has 450 branches among Irish communities in countries outside
Ireland.

See also Fleadh Cheoil

C

Communion Tokens

A tradition that exists within the Presbyterian church in which tokens are handed out to members of the congregation and then returned when that person has received Holy Communion. This practice was adopted because Presbyterian procedure dictates that a person is not entitled to vote at congregational meetings unless they are a communicant. A communion roll book is kept by the kirk session and a person's name is entered into it every time they return a token after receiving Holy Communion. In early times the tokens were made of metal and minted locally, but nowadays they are almost always made of card. The cards are handed out by elders perhaps a week before Holy Communion is due to take place, although in stricter times a card might have been withheld if the elders were not sufficiently convinced of the sincerity of that person's Christian belief, or if they had not paid all their congregational dues.

See also Holy Communion, Kirk Session, Ruling Elder

Concertina

Said to have been invented by Englishman Charles Wheatstone in 1825, and originally called a symphonium, the concertina belongs to the free-reed family of instruments, in which the sound is produced by air vibrations on a series of metal strips. With the concertina, pressing keys on either side of the instrument allows air to pass over the reeds. The distinctive hexagonal instrument probably developed around the end of the eighteenth century and while it has enjoyed a fair degree of popularity throughout Ireland, it has always been most favoured among musicians in County Clare.

See also Accordion

Confirmation

A ceremony carried out within most churches which celebrate the Eucharist (Holy

Communion). In the majority of cases, a candidate who has been previously baptised undergoes confirmation when they are in their teenage years. In the Church of Ireland, parishioners can only receive Holy Communion once they have been confirmed, whereas in the Catholic church children receive their first Holy Communion at the age of seven and are confirmed at around ten years of age. In both churches the ceremony is carried out by the bishop of the diocese. Within the Presbyterian and Methodist churches members do not receive full Communion until they have been confirmed by the local minister.

See also Catholic Church, Church of Ireland, First Communion, Holy Communion, Methodist Church, Presbyterian Church

Conradh na Gaeilge *see* Gaelic League

Convent

The term 'convent' can be applied not only to the building in which members of a religious order live, but also to the religious community itself. The word is taken from the Latin word *conventus*, meaning 'meeting'. In past times a convent could refer to both male and female religious orders, although today it is almost always applied to a female order, and in Ireland is mostly associated with the Catholic faith.

See also Nun

Corpus Christi

A Catholic feast day, usually in June, which was formerly marked by a carnival-style public procession and is still often celebrated in the same way, although now generally on a smaller scale and sometimes held only within church grounds. The feast centres around the Catholic doctrine of transubstantiation – the belief that Christ's presence in the bread and wine of the Eucharist is not symbolic but real. At the time of the

C

feast's initiation in the
thirteenth century, there
was much debate within
the Catholic church about
this belief, but it is said
that when a doubting
bishop broke bread for
the Eucharist a drop of
blood appeared from it.
This story led to a
revival of traditional faith
and the feast of Corpus
Christi ('the body of

Christ') was founded. The development of the procession to
accompany the feast allowed the faithful to publicly express their
adherence to the belief.

See also Holy Communion,
Sacred Heart of Jesus

County

Based on the English system
of land division into shires, where the monarch's authority was
represented by a sheriff, counties were gradually introduced into
Ireland over a period of several centuries following the arrival of the
Normans. The aim was to divide the country into a series of easily
administered blocks with prominent natural features, such as rivers,
serving as the boundaries. Down and Antrim were among the first
regions of Ulster to be considered counties, as they were the main
part of the Norman earldom of Ulster, although it was a number of
centuries before a complete county system for the whole of Ireland
was in place. Most of the counties were named after prominent
towns within their boundaries, with the exceptions of Tyrone and
Fermanagh in Ulster, which were named after people. County
Londonderry was known as the county of Coleraine up until early-
seventeenth-century plantation times, when the area was granted to
London companies and the county border was redrawn.

See also Barony, Parish,
Plantation, Province, Townland,
Ulster

C

Crack

A word which originated in Scotland, where it is often spelt craik, but is not as widely used there as it is in Ireland. Crack means literally 'speech', 'talk' or even 'gossip', but it has also come to mean entertaining conversation or good fun in general. The word crack has been brought into the modern Irish language as *craic*, a spelling that is becoming increasingly common.

Crannog

An artificial island built in a shallow lake or marshland which was used either as an easily defended dwelling place or as a refuge in times of attack. Built of stones, timber or peat, the islands were usually surrounded by wooden defence walls and many also had wicker houses built on them. The earliest crannogs date back to the latter years of the Bronze Age and they continued to be a popular form of defensive position up until the Middle Ages.

C

Cricket

No one can say with any authority when the game of cricket was first invented, but it seems very likely that it shares the same origins as the bat-and-ball games of hurling, hockey and shinty. Cricket came to Ireland some time in the eighteenth century, brought across the Irish Sea by the military, the gentry and English civil servants. The first recorded match in Ireland took place in the Phoenix Park, Dublin, in 1792, between a team called the Garrison, captained by a future lord lieutenant, Lieutenant Colonel Charles Lennox, and a team incorrectly titled All-Ireland, led by a future secretary of war, Major Robert Hobart. It is said that 1,000 guineas was wagered on the result of the game. The first Irish cricket club was formed in the 1820s, and the club with the highest membership, North of Ireland Cricket Club in Belfast, was founded in 1859. The sport was largely dominated by the gentry and the military at this time and many clubs were based in garrison towns around Ireland. Surprisingly, the sport initially proved very popular in counties Galway, Carlow and Kilkenny, which are now hurling and Gaelic football heartlands. The Irish Cricket Union was formed in 1923 but the sport was fairly moribund until the mid-1960s when a revival in its fortunes was heralded by the inauguration of a new inter-provincial cup and the creation of several junior tournaments. There are now around 130 cricket clubs in Ireland, the majority in the eastern half of the island. On the international scene, Ireland's finest hour took place amid the outbreak of open sectarian conflict in the North in 1969 when its national cricket side dismissed the mighty West Indies for just twenty-five runs in a game at Sion Mills, County Tyrone.

See also Hockey, Hurling, Rugby, Shinty

C

Cruthin

An ancient people who, numerically, dominated eastern Ulster and were scattered across other parts of Ireland in pre-Christian times. It is claimed that the Cruthin lived in Ireland before the gradual arrival of the Celts in the first millennium BC, and their customs and lifestyle, which were similar to many other tribes in Ireland, persisted for some centuries before being overwhelmed by the powerful influence of Celtic culture. It has been argued that the Cruthin shared a similar ethnic background with peoples on the other side of the Irish Sea, where they were called Pretani (after whom Britain is named). When the Romans came to Britain they made a wider distinction between the inhabitants of the islands by rechristening the Pretani 'Picti' and labelling the Irish 'Scotti'. Many of the Scotti travelled from Ireland across the North Channel to settle in what would later become known as Scotland, and it is claimed that a significant proportion of the Scotti settlers were Cruthin people, as were the indigenous Picti. A continuation of the theory suggests that the planters who came to Ulster from Scotland in the seventeenth century could well have been the descendants of Cruthin who came from Ireland in the first place. Many of these ideas and arguments are hotly disputed within academic circles, but neither side appears to have any concrete evidence to confirm or disprove the theories.

See also Celts, Plantation

Cú Chulainn

One of the central figures of the mythic Ulster Cycle of Tales, Cú Chulainn was originally named Setanta. As a young man, he came to the attention of the king of

Ulster, Culann, after defeating 150 opponents at wrestling. The king invited Setanta to feast with him at his home on the slopes of Slieve Gullion, but when the young man arrived at the house he discovered that the entrance was guarded by a savage dog. The animal leapt to attack Setanta, but he grabbed it by the throat and struck its head against a stone pillar, killing it. The king was pleased that Setanta was unharmed, but now his home was left without a guard dog, so Setanta agreed to take the dog's place until a puppy from the same pack could be trained to take his place. From this time on he was renamed Cú Chulainn, which means the 'hound of Culann', and in the years that followed he also became known as the 'hound of Ulster', a mighty warrior who performed many feats of bravery.

See also Cattle Raid of Cooley, Celts, Navan Fort, Ulster Cycle of Tales

Curate

A term used both in the Catholic church and the Church of Ireland to describe a clergyman who assists the parish priest or the rector. The word curate is linked to the phrase 'cure of souls', an archaic term for the pastoral care of souls in the parish.

See also Catholic Church, Church of Ireland, Parish, Priest, Rector

C

Cures

There are two distinct types of cure prevalent in Ireland. One is freely passed on – such as the belief that carrying a potato in your pocket will cure rheumatism, or a stye will be cured by rubbing it with a gold wedding ring – while the other is a closely guarded secret, known only to a select few. What both types of cure require, however, is a strong belief by the recipient that they will actually work, since most have no scientific or rational justification. But that does not stop many today seeking out people in their locality who are known to have a cure for a particular ailment. Some cures may involve special prayers, others might consist of secret ointments or drinks. There are also many customs associated with cures – a recipient might be told not to thank the curer because it would destroy the charm, and many who know the secret of a cure say they cannot reveal it because then it would no longer work. Those who possess the cures obtain their powers by a variety of means. A married woman whose maiden name was the same as her husband's surname will often have a cure, as will a child whose parents had the same surname before marriage, or a son whose father died before he was born. Perhaps the best-known possessor of the power to cure is the seventh son of a seventh son. Holy wells are also a source of cures, though once again the emphasis is as much on faith as it is on any special powers the waters may have.

C

Defenders

A Catholic faction formed during the sectarian warfare that flared in County Armagh in the 1780s. Carried out in response to attacks on Catholic homes by the Protestant Peep o' Day Boys, the Defenders' campaign was similarly vicious, culminating in the notorious murder and mutilation of a Forkhill schoolmaster and his wife. Better-organised, though not as well-armed as their Protestant rivals, the Defenders created a network of clubs and established oaths of allegiance. Seen by some as the forerunners of the United Irishmen, the Defenders were at least partly influenced by revolutionary thinking in France and America, although their agenda was undeniably sectarian.

See also Ancient Order of Hibernians, Peep o' Day Boys, United Irishmen

Deirdre of the Sorrows

A story from the Ulster Cycle of Tales which tells of the daughter of one of the Red Branch knights whose birth was accompanied by a prediction that she would be a great beauty who would marry a king but would also bring death and destruction to the province of Ulster. When the king of Ulster, Conchobar MacNessa, heard this prediction he vowed to marry Deirdre so that no foreign king would threaten his land. However, as Deirdre grew up, she fell in love with a handsome young courtier called Naoise and eventually the pair eloped to Scotland with the aid of Naoise's two brothers. Seeking revenge for the insult, King Conchobar sent a trusted messenger, Fergus, to tell the exiles that all was forgiven and they were welcome to return to Ulster. Upon their return, Naoise and his two brothers were slain and Deirdre committed suicide after being ordered by King Conchobar to live with the man who had killed her love and his brothers. Fergus, who had been unaware that his mission was a ruse, reacted furiously and swore that none of

Conchobar's family would succeed to the throne of Ulster. He joined the army of Queen Medbh of Connacht and some time later returned with a force which ravaged Ulster and laid waste to Conchobar's seat of power, Emain Macha (Navan Fort).

See also Cattle Raid of Cooley, Navan Fort, Red Branch Knights, Ulster Cycle of Tales

Demesne

A word derived from Norman French describing land attached to a landlord's estate which is retained for his own use, rather than rented out to tenants. Despite having fallen into disuse in England, the term can still be found in many parts of Ireland, where the word is often incorrectly used to refer to the manicured parkland surrounding country houses. In fact, a demesne would have covered a much larger area, encompassing grazing lands, cultivated fields and other features such as a deer park or an orchard.

See also Normans

Diaspora

A term originally used to describe the dispersion of Jews among Gentile nations which has now been widened to refer to descendants of emigrants from a particular country. The Irish diaspora is particularly widespread, due in part to the fact that few emigrants returned to their native land once they had left. It has been estimated that some 70 million people worldwide now claim Irish descent.

D

See also Emigration

Dolmen

Also known as portal tombs or cromlechs, these distinctive megalithic monuments are found more often in Ulster than in any other province in Ireland. They usually consist of three stone pillars supporting a flat boulder, or capstone, and were built to mark the graves of individuals or families. Some of the most impressive examples of dolmens are in County Down, at Legananny and Goward in the Mournes. The dolmen at Ballylumford, County Antrim, is now part of someone's front garden.

Drumlin

A small hill formed by boulder clay scraped from the Ulster hills by glaciers during the last ice age in Ireland. A belt of drumlins stretches from the County Down coast in the east to Donegal Bay in the west, providing a natural barrier between north and south that was accentuated by the construction of the Black Pig's Dyke and other fortifications in pre-Christian times. The word drumlin is the anglicisation of an Irish term meaning 'little hill'. 'Drum' is a common prefix for towns and villages situated within the south Ulster drumlin belt.

D

See also Black Pig's Dyke

Easter Lily

The association of the Easter lily with republicanism dates back to the Easter Rising of 1916. The lily was a common seasonal decoration in churches at the time of the rising, but it was not until 1926 that it began to be worn on the lapel as a flower of remembrance for those who had died for the cause of Irish independence. The wearing of the lily is central to the origin of the term 'stickie', which is widely used to describe supporters and members of the Official IRA since its split with the Provisional IRA in 1970. The story goes that Official IRA supporters tended to wear Easter lilies with a self-adhesive backing on their coat lapels at Easter Rising commemorations, while Provisional supporters used a traditional pin to secure their lilies.

See also Easter Rising, Republicanism

Easter Rising

Following the derailment of the Irish home rule campaign by World War I, nationalist frustration at the thwarting of movement towards independence boiled over into armed insurrection on the streets of Dublin in April 1916. Nationalist sentiment had been stirred by the 1898 centenary commemoration of the United Irishmen's rebellion, which had also given new energy to the military agenda of the Irish Republican Brotherhood (IRB) and coincided with the turn-of-the-century Gaelic cultural revival. The rising began on

Easter Monday when five battalions of the IRB, totalling 1,800 men, commanded by Patrick Pearse, and 200 men of the socialist Irish Citizen Army under James Connolly took up central positions at the General Post Office in Dublin and declared the establishment of the Irish Republic. Six days later, after prolonged street fighting and the death of 450 people, Pearse and Connolly signed an unconditional surrender. Their execution, along with those of thirteen other key figures in the rising, led to a widespread outpouring of public sympathy and elevated the leaders to the status of martyrs. At the beginning of the rising public opinion had been largely against the insurgents – many believed it was a German-inspired plot – but following the executions the national mood changed sharply to one of wholehearted support for the drive towards independence.

See also Easter Lily, Fenians, Home Rule, Republicanism, Starry Plough, United Irishmen

Ecumenism

A movement which aims to reconcile the differences between Christian churches and unite Christians of all denominations. Ecumenism is seen by its opponents as an attempt to destroy the traditions and doctrines of the differing churches, while its supporters believe that it is God's will that all Christian churches should be united. Although the roots of this aspiration can be found within the New Testament, ecumenism did not develop into a potent force until the twentieth century. Following an initial ecumenical thrust from within Protestantism, the movement was encouraged by the Second Vatican Council's decree on ecumenism in 1964, which significantly described the non-Roman churches as 'separated brethren'. This was followed by the foundation of the Irish School of Ecumenics in 1970. The ultimate objective of a single unified Christian church may seem to be unattainable, but the spirit of ecumenism has led to closer dialogue and co-operation between the various churches.

E

Éire

The Irish language name for Ireland. When the Celts displaced the Tuatha Dé Danaan and drove them underground, Ériu was one of three goddesses who extracted a promise from the victors that the land would some day bear her name. A visionary poet pledged that Ériu's name would be given to the land, providing that she ensured Ireland would belong to the Celts for ever. The Irish Free State was officially renamed Éire in 1937, a name which was retained until a republic was declared in 1949.

See also Celts, Free State, Tuatha Dé Danaan

Elder *see* Ruling Elder

Emain Macha *see* Navan Fort

Emigration

The large number of songs, stories and poems about the heartbreak of enforced emigration has often tended to obscure the fact that not all emigrants from Ireland left unwillingly. In the early eighteenth century a large number of Ulster Presbyterians left for the American colonies because their dissenting religion barred them from public office and there were many opportunities for advancement on the other side of the Atlantic. As many as 250,000 people from Ulster had settled in

E

America by the time the revolution broke out in 1775, and a number of them were to play leading roles in the insurrection (it is said that one in four of all US presidents have Irish roots). The more traditional picture of Irish emigration emerged during the Famine years when over one million people departed the country to escape poverty and starvation. Forty per cent of those who emigrated in the period 1847–8 were from Ulster. Many went to Britain, America and Canada, while some went to Australia either as convicts or emigrants. Though the numbers leaving Ireland peaked around the time of the Famine, emigration continued on a large scale well into the twentieth century, and in the seventy years up to 1911 the population of Ulster fell by more than one-third. Significantly, most of those who emigrated, and their descendants, never returned to live in Ireland.

See also Diaspora, Famine

Eucharist *see* Holy Communion, Mass

Evangelism

A school of religious thinking which energetically promotes Christian conversion and personal salvation through the power of faith, rather than through the sacraments of the church or good works. Evangelism is widely associated with the Protestant churches, and although it is not the preserve of any single church, a number of churches in Ireland have embarked on evangelical revivals to renew the spiritual life of its congregations and attract new members. Evangelism was a prominent force in the Church of Ireland at the beginning of the nineteenth century, and by the middle of the century Presbyterian evangelism was at its peak, particularly in 1859, which was dubbed the 'year of grace'. The word evangelist comes from a Greek phrase meaning 'proclaimer of good news', highlighting the great emphasis placed upon the teachings of the Bible in evangelism. The term originally applied to a travelling missionary who would also have held a church post, but today it more commonly refers to a

E

layperson within a Protestant church who undertakes popular preaching. Examples of evangelistic outreach in Northern Ireland include week-long 'tent missions' in specially erected marquees or outdoor praise services at seaside resorts.

See also Methodism, Protestantism

Extreme Unction *see* Unction

Fáinne

An award for oral proficiency in the Irish Language. *Fáinne* means 'ring' and is so called because the lapel badge presented for achievement is ring-shaped. There are three levels of *fáinne* – the learner's, the silver and the gold.

See also Irish Language

Famine

The potato famine of 1845–50, also widely known as the Great Famine, was not the only time when crop failures in Ireland led to widespread starvation and death, but these years were certainly the most devastating. Over one million people died and a further million emigrated, the first massive wave in a tide of emigration that cut Ireland's population in half by the end of the century. The worst effects of the Famine were felt in the western half of Ireland, where starvation, bitter winters and fevers took an appalling toll. In the eastern half of the country the northern counties were hit harder than the prosperous lands around Dublin and it is estimated that the Famine accounted for at least a quarter of a million Ulster deaths. Starvation drove the worst-affected to desperate acts – drinking the blood of animals to survive, raiding food stores, boarding crowded, ill-equipped ships for a hazardous emigration passage – but an uprising by the Young Ireland movement in 1848, the fiftieth anniversary of the United Irishmen's rebellion, failed to find popular support and floundered after one minor skirmish. Official relief measures in most parts of the country

F

were unable to cope with the scale of the disaster. Workhouses, funded by poor rates collected from local property owners, were overflowing and teetering on the edge of bankruptcy as landowners baulked at the prospect of footing their soaring bills. Eventually outdoor relief, in the form of soup kitchens, was provided by official and voluntary groups. Some soup kitchens were run by proselytising Protestant churches who insisted that recipients changed their religion before they were given food – a practice known derisively as 'taking the soup' – although many gave food freely. A decision to prematurely withdraw the official soup kitchens in 1847 proved to be another disastrous step in the hopelessly inadequate government response to the widespread starvation, and even when the government declared that the Famine was over, people continued to die in their thousands. It was only due to the safety valve of emigration that the final toll was not considerably higher.

See also Diaspora, Emigration, Potato, Quakers

Feis

Feis is the name given to a number of different cultural competitions involving the Irish language, traditional music and Irish dancing. The *Feis Cheoil* is a music and singing competition set up by the Gaelic League at the turn of the century and there is also an Irish language *feis* for the spoken word and an Irish dancing *feis*, which are separate competitions altogether. In this context the word *feis* means 'entertainment' although it is also an early Irish word for sexual intercourse.

See also Gaelic League

Fenians

In 1858 a secret organisation (later known as the Irish Republican Brotherhood) was founded in Dublin by James Stephens, one of the survivors of a failed rebellion by the Young Ireland movement ten years previously. A parallel

F

body, the Fenian Brotherhood, was founded in New York the following year by John O'Mahony. The movement recruited and obtained secret oaths of allegiance from several thousand people and a considerable number of soldiers who had fought in the American Civil War came to Ireland in 1865 when that war ended. However, an uprising in 1867 failed because of internal divisions in the organisation, betrayal by informers and prompt police action. Queen Victoria was sufficiently impressed by the work of the Irish police that she renamed them the 'Royal' Irish Constabulary. In the months that followed the failed rising, spectacular jailbreak attempts by Fenian prisoners in England, which resulted in a number of deaths, focused the mind of Liberal leader, William Gladstone, on the need for reform in Ireland. The IRB, meanwhile, continued to survive as an organisation in the twentieth century, but was eclipsed by the IRA after the Easter Rising of 1916.

See also Easter Rising, Famine

Fiddle

The fiddle is one of the most popular instruments for playing Irish traditional music, mainly because of its flexibility as an instrument and its suitability for dance music. It began to be commonly used in Ireland around the second half of the seventeenth century and over the years distinctive playing styles developed in different regions of Ireland. The most notable regional styles are those found in Donegal, Sligo, Clare and the Sliabh Luachra area of County Kerry.

First Communion

A Catholic ceremony in which children receive Holy Communion for the first time. The children usually receive First Communion at the age of seven, having already made their first confession. The age of seven was historically judged by the church to be the age of reason, when a child was able to understand the significance of the ceremony. Traditionally, girls receiving their First Communion dress in white, which symbolises innocence and also has echoes of the early Christians who wore white as a sign of their new life in Christ. First Communion ceremonies are usually conducted in May by the parish priest and children take part with members of their school class.

See also Confirmation, Holy Communion, Parish Priest

Fleadh Cheoil

A weekend of music competitions and informal sessions organised by Comhaltas Ceoltóirí Éireann, which usually goes under the more simplified name of a *fleadh* (*fleadh cheoil* means 'music festival'). Competitors demonstrate their skills in singing and musicianship in a range of different age categories in the formal part of the festival, and there are also open air sessions and get-togethers of musicians in local pubs, which can often continue until dawn. *Fleadh* winners at county level proceed to the provincial finals and then aim for a place in the all-Ireland finals. Competitors from similar *fleadhanna* in Britain and the United States also take part in the finals. Since the first all-Ireland *fleadh* in 1953, the festival has grown enormously.

F

The 1997 *fleadh* in Ballina, County Mayo, attracted over 10,000 musicians and some 150,000 visitors.

See also Comhaltas Ceoltóirí Éireann

Flight of the Earls

The symbolic end of the old Gaelic order in Ulster took place on the shores of Lough Swilly in 1607 when Hugh O'Neill, Earl of Tyrone, and around one hundred fellow nobles, family members and followers fled Ireland for Europe. Ulster was the last of the Gaelic provinces to hold out against increasing sixteenth-century English domination of Ireland; most Irish chieftains had already pledged allegiance to the English crown and accepted the rule of English law. In 1585 O'Neill was granted the title of Earl of Tyrone by Elizabeth I on the understanding that he too would accept English law and introduce it throughout Ulster. Instead he clung to the Gaelic way of life and resisted all attempts to force him to change. Tensions eventually escalated into nine years of open warfare in which O'Neill won a number of early victories but was eventually defeated by English forces at the Battle of Kinsale in 1601. Allowed to keep his lands providing he introduced English law, O'Neill nonetheless found himself in a precarious position. His power was weakened, there were those who felt he had been dealt with too leniently after Kinsale, and assassination seemed ever more likely. Within months of the departure of O'Neill and his followers, their lands were confiscated by the crown and the way was open for the wholesale plantation of Ulster.

See also Celts, Plantation

Flute

The tradition of flute bands in Ireland arose from the military fife and drum corps maintained in garrison towns throughout the country in the eighteenth and ninteenth centuries. Irishmen who joined the army often learned to play the fife (a simple keyless wooden instrument with a high-pitched tone) and later brought their skills to local bands which

F

grew up independently of the army in the nineteenth century. Contrary to popular perception, these new bands were not solely tied to the Orange tradition. Though some Orange lodges had their own band, many other flute bands were totally independent; some were linked to the Ancient Order of Hibernians and the Irish National Foresters while others were attached to political groupings, such as the Conservatives or Land League movement. During the course of the twentieth century, however, the number of flute bands outside the Orange tradition gradually declined. Meanwhile, the fife was superseded by the one-key flute, which increased the range of music a band could play and ushered in the tradition of 'melody' bands, also known as 'first flute' or 'principal' bands. These bands simply played the tune rather than dividing into harmonic sections. However, more complex arrangements became possible with the introduction of the four-, five- and six-key flutes and improvements in flute construction. Many bands began to include a variety of different flutes in their line-up and played music which was arranged into parts. In 1947 the Flute Band League of Northern Ireland was formed and the winner of its premier competition today is acknowledged as the world champion flute band. It has been estimated that there are currently around one thousand flute bands in Northern Ireland, ranging from the casual melody band – which may only perform in public on the Twelfth of July each year – to the remarkably high standard of the concert flute band. Flute bands are still in existence in former garrison towns in the Irish Republic, such as Limerick, Waterford and Wexford; there is also a strong tradition centred around Glasgow, and similar bands exist in Canada and the United States. Within Irish traditional music circles, the flute became a popular instrument with players around the end of the nineteenth

F

century. It is particularly associated with traditional musicians in counties Sligo, Roscommon and Leitrim.

See also Ancient Order of Hibernians, Irish National Foresters, Orange Order, Tin Whistle, Twelfth of July

Free Presbyterian Church of Ulster

Founded by the Reverend Ian Paisley in 1951 during a gospel revivalist campaign in Northern Ireland, the first Free Presbyterian church was established in Crossgar, County Down, after a dispute with the Presbyterian church over the use of its facilities for Dr Paisley's gospel meetings. In the years that followed a number of disaffected Presbyterians and others were attracted by the fundamentalist philosophy of the Free Presbyterian church. In the period from 1970 to 1983 some twenty-eight new churches were built, and today there are around one hundred Free Presbyterian churches in Northern Ireland, the Republic of Ireland, England, North America, Australia, Jamaica and Spain. Dr Paisley's Martyrs' Memorial church in south Belfast was, at the time of building, one of the largest Protestant churches in Europe. In 1991 there were around 12,500 members of the church, making it the seventh largest denomination in Northern Ireland. The emblem of the Free Presbyterian church incorporates the burning bush of Presbyterianism and the motto 'Christ for Ulster'.

See also Burning Bush, Presbyterian Church, Protestantism

Free State

The southern twenty-six counties of Ireland became the Irish Free State after the signing of the Anglo-Irish Treaty on 6 December 1921. The treaty had been drawn up after the War of Independence (1919–21) but it did not grant full independence to Ireland; the newly created state was still a

F

dominion of the British Empire, similar in status to Canada. This halfway house arrangement sparked a civil war in southern Ireland, in which the republican anti-treaty forces were defeated by the Free State army in 1923. Southern Ireland ceased to be known as the Irish Free State when it became a republic in 1949.

See also Éire, Home Rule, Partition, Republicanism

Freemasons

Freemasonry in Ireland encompasses a series of inter-linked organisations, each with its own complex series of rituals, regalia and symbols of significance. The Order of Ancient, Free and Accepted Masons of Ireland is based upon the guild system which developed in medieval times. Guilds were groups of skilled craftsmen or traders who banded together for mutual benefit and taught new members the secrets of their craft over a period of apprenticeship. The Freemasons are based around the concept of a guild of builders and much of their symbolism and ritual derives from the biblical building of Solomon's Temple in Jerusalem. A new mason graduates through three 'craft' degrees of seniority from Entered Apprentice to Fellow Craft to Master Mason. He may also become initiated into related organisations, such as the Royal Arch (which draws its symbolism from the repair of Solomon's Temple) or the Order of the Temple, which differs from the guild structure in that it is based on orders of chivalry and is inspired by the defence of Jerusalem and the temple. The Ancient Accepted Scottish Rite of Heredom is a separate series of thirty-three degrees which only the dedicated few ever complete. In practice, all candidates commence at the eighteenth degree and few progress beyond the twenty-eighth degree. The earliest evidence

F

of freemasonry in Ireland dates back to the late seventeenth century and the governing Grand Lodge was formed in 1725. Although the order is essentially non-sectarian in nature, the majority of its members have tended to be Protestant. The Catholic church was hostile to freemasonry in the nineteenth century partly because the liberal attitudes of the order were in conflict with the church's more conservative outlook. As a result, Catholics were forbidden to join the masons and Daniel O'Connell, the nineteenth-century champion of Catholic Emancipation, was among those forced to resign. Many Protestant churches also oppose freemasonry, particularly the more evangelical churches, who argue that masonic interpretation of portions of the Bible is embellished and not based strictly upon the text. Some opponents have also expressed concerns about the 'secret' nature of freemasonry, although members maintain that they have a right to privacy.

See also Knights of Malta, Royal Arch Purple

F

Gael

Gael is derived from the early Celtic word *goidel*, which can be interpreted as meaning a 'wild man of the woods'. Some authorities say that the Goidels were a Celtic tribe which settled in Ireland around 1000 BC, while others maintain that this term was simply a disparaging description of the Irish used by early Christian missionaries from Britain. The most common modern definition of a Gael is an Irish or Scottish person of Celtic descent.

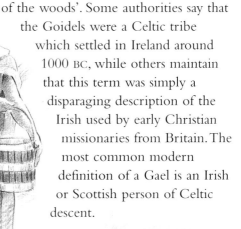

See also Celts

Gaelic Athletic Association

The sports that have become known as Gaelic games were in existence in Ireland long before the formation of the Gaelic Athletic Association (GAA) in 1884, but there were different rules for the various games in different parts of Ireland. Before the GAA brought in their own standardised rules, teams would meet before a match and agree rules for that particular game. The association was founded during a Gaelic cultural revival in Ireland by Michael Cusack, Maurice Davin and Archbishop Thomas William Croke (after whom Croke Park in Dublin is named). The organisation's influence was initially slow to spread in Ulster; it was not until the 1920s that the GAA was established in County Fermanagh and a decade later before it was formally inaugurated in County Londonderry. However, an Ulster county, Antrim, was the beaten finalist in the first all-Ireland county competition in 1911. Since its formation the GAA has used Catholic

G

parishes as the basis for its organisational structure. Each parish has its own club which organises a variety of Gaelic games, including football, hurling, camogie and, to a lesser extent, handball and rounders. Parish clubs compete in county leagues and also in all-Ireland club championships at minor, junior and senior level. Exceptional players at club level may be selected to play for their county team, which competes in an all-Ireland league, the National Football League (NFL), or NHL in the case of hurling. There is also a knockout championship in which county teams compete at a provincial level, and the four provincial winners battle it out for the all-Ireland title. In addition to the promotion of Gaelic games, the GAA has a strong cultural emphasis through the promotion of *Scór* competitions and its encouragement of the Irish language. It is currently estimated that there are over one million registered members of the GAA in Ireland.

See also Camogie, Gaelic Football, Handball, Hurling, Irish Language, Rugby, Scór, Soccer

Gaelic Football

To the followers of Gaelic games, the term 'football' is generally taken to refer to Gaelic football, while association football is referred to as soccer. The widespread use of the word football as a colloquial term for both sports is an indication of the common origins of Gaelic football and soccer, both of which developed from a boisterous inter-village or parish field game played to locally agreed rules. Gaelic football gained its separate identity with the drawing up of official rules following the formation of the GAA in 1884. The number of players in a team was initially standardised at 25, although this was reduced some time later to 21, and finally, in the 1930s, to 15 a side. A Gaelic football match today consists of two halves of

G

35 minutes each, reduced from the original 80 minutes' duration of a game (although matches were shortened to 60 minutes for a time). Scores are made in two ways: by hitting the ball over the crossbar between the uprights to score a point, and by hitting the ball under the crossbar between the uprights to score a goal, which is worth three points. It is possible, therefore, for a team that has not scored a goal during a match to beat opponents who may have scored a number of goals. In an effort to internationalise the game, Gaelic footballers from Ireland have played challenge matches with Australian Rules football teams under agreed 'compromise rules', which are a composite of the rules of the two organisations. (It is thought that Australian Rules football is itself derived from the Gaelic version of football brought to the Antipodes by Irish emigrants and transported convicts.) Gaelic football teams can also be found in many major English and American cities. The players in a New York team which recently participated in an all-Ireland minor football championship were all American-born and some of them were not even of Irish descent.

See also Gaelic Athletic Association, Rugby, Soccer

Gaelic League

The Gaelic League (in Irish, *Conradh na Gaeilge*) was founded in 1893 by Douglas Hyde, a Protestant scholar who became the first president of Ireland in 1938, and by Eoin MacNeill, a historian who was later chief of staff in the breakaway Irish Volunteers. The league was created during a period of Gaelic cultural revival which also saw the formation of the Gaelic Athletic Association. The Irish language had been showing signs of marked decline at this time and the main aim of the Gaelic League was to encourage more people to both learn and use it. Although the first Ulster branch was established in Belfast in 1895, initial enthusiasm for its work was more muted in northern counties than elsewhere in Ireland. Nevertheless, its initial attempts to be non-political earned the league a broad cross-section of support; among those who took an active part in the early days of the organisation were the Grand Master of the Belfast Orange Lodge and the Grand

G

Master of the Independent Orange Order. But this gradually changed as the league was perceived to be aligning itself more closely with Irish nationalist movements in the years preceding the Easter Rising. The Gaelic League still plays a prominent role in the promotion of the Irish language today, providing classes and organising events throughout Ireland.

See also Gaelic Athletic
Association, Irish Language

Gaeltacht

Gaeltacht literally means 'gaeldom' and it describes an area where the community uses the Irish language in daily life. *Gaeltacht* areas in Ireland are mostly located along the west coast, from Donegal to Kerry, and each area will be home to at least one language school. West Belfast is the only *Gaeltacht* in Northern Ireland and the only urban *Gaeltacht* in the Gaelic-speaking world.

See also Irish Language

General Assembly

The most senior body within the Presbyterian church in Ireland, but even this grouping does not have the executive power to change the constitution of the church, such is the rigorous system of accountability in the Presbyterian church. The General Assembly meets for a week in June each year and anything up to 1,200 elders and ministers may attend, although the number is usually much less than this. All its boards and committees are made up of balanced numbers of ministers and elders and no person can hold an appointment on any of these boards for more than nine years, to prevent cliques forming. During

G

the week of the General Assembly, a moderator will be elected and issues of importance to the church will be discussed. Any major decisions passed by a majority at the General Assembly, however, have to be approved by a majority of the presbyteries at local level before they can be effected.

See also Moderator, Presbyterian Church, Presbytery, Ruling Elders

Gerrymander

A term named after Governor Elbridge Gerry of Massachusetts, whose constituency manipulations earned him notoriety in the US elections of 1812. It is unclear when the term first came to be used in Northern Ireland, but the practice of a political grouping altering constituency boundaries to give it increased representation dates back to the years immediately following partition in 1921. The unwillingness of nationalists to co-operate with the drawing up of local government boundaries in 1922–3 (because they refused to recognise the new state) gave unionists a free hand to create electoral areas that gave them maximum advantage in an election, with the result that in the 1927 local election unionists had a majority in 15 out of 27 councils. A majority in the local council meant control over public housing and in a number of areas this led to discrimination against Catholics seeking council houses. Gerrymandering and its consequences were one of the main reasons for the formation of the Northern Ireland Civil Rights Association in 1968.

See also Civil Rights Movement, Partition

Giant's Causeway

One of the best-known features of the natural landscape in Ireland, the Giant's Causeway is made up of thousands of hexagonal and polygonal pillars formed by the cooling of lava which burst through the earth's crust in the Cainozoic period of pre-history. There are many tales and legends

G

associated with the causeway, most notably those connected with Finn Mac Cool. The causeway is so named because there are traces of similar rock formations at Staffa on the Isle of Skye, suggesting a mythical land-bridge between Scotland and Ireland. The Irish name for the causeway is *Clochan na bhFomharaigh*, which means 'stepping stones of the Fomorii'. The Fomorii were reputed to be a violent race of often hideously disfigured people whose home was thought to be Tory Island, off the Donegal coast. Some of the Fomorii were also said to have been abnormally tall

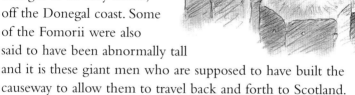

and it is these giant men who are supposed to have built the causeway to allow them to travel back and forth to Scotland.

Glór na nGael

An all-Ireland competition, which in English means 'voice of the Gael', to encourage communities to promote the Irish language. Prizes are awarded each year to towns and villages which have done the most to encourage the use of the language.

See also Gael, Irish language

G

Hail Mary

A prayer drawn from Saint Luke's account of the birth of Jesus which is commonly used within the Catholic church. The full text of the short prayer is:

Hail Mary, full of grace,
The Lord is with thee.
Blessed art thou amongst women
And blessed is the fruit of thy womb, Jesus.

Holy Mary, Mother of God,
Pray for us sinners
Now and at the hour of our death. Amen.

See also Rosary

Hallowe'en

The word Hallowe'en is derived from All Hallows' Eve, the night before the Christian feast of All Saints' Day on 1 November. However, the traditions associated with Hallowe'en extend to pre-Christian times and have their roots in the Celtic festival of *Samhain*, which marked the end of summer and the onset of the dark months of winter. It was believed that the souls of the dead returned to walk the earth on the last day of summer. Bonfires were an integral feature of the occasion, perhaps to light the way for the souls of loved ones or else to keep evil at bay. The later introduction of fireworks, invented by the Chinese to ward off malevolent spirits, may be an extension of this idea. Hallowe'en was also believed to be a time when it was possible to see into the future, and a number of customs centre around divining one's future prosperity or love life. Explanations for many of the traditions differ: for example, some say

H

that ducking for apples was a prediction of marriage, and the first to bite an apple would be married within the year, while others claim that the bigger the apple bitten by the participant, the more prosperous they would be in later life. In keeping with the idea of seeing into the future, it is said that a child born on 31 October as the clock is striking midnight will be endowed with second sight.

See also Samhain

Handball

Handball is a game played throughout the world and administered in Ireland by the GAA. Similar to squash, it is played by two participants who hit a ball against a wall with the flat of their hands rather than with a racket. Initially, a handball court consisted of only one wall, but later developments led to the creation of the 'open alley' with three walls and the fully enclosed 'box alley'. There are pockets of interest in the sport in Ulster and elsewhere in Ireland (particularly Kilkenny) but widespread support for handball has been waning over the years.

See also Gaelic Athletic Association

Harp

The earliest known depiction of one of Ireland's national symbols is to be found not in Ireland but in Scotland, where representations of the instrument were etched on to stone crosses as far back as the eighth century AD. The earliest known depiction in Ireland was created some three hundred years later. However, the harp was clearly well-known in Ireland by this time and there were many expert players in the twelfth century. Chieftains often had their own personal harper and music performed on the instrument was generally enjoyed more by the rulers than the ruled. Gradually, harp music came to be perceived as anti-English, and in 1366 there was an attempt to ban the playing of it within the Pale around Dublin. When this failed, the English

H

attempted to absorb the harp into its own heraldic symbolism and the instrument was featured on Irish coins (underneath a crown) and state documents. It was even included in the royal arms in 1603, and still remains there. One of the most significant events in the history of the harp as a musical instrument in Ireland was the Belfast Harp Festival of 1792. In the centuries prior to this, Ireland had a strong tradition of the itinerant harper – a musician who travelled the countryside playing for his living – but by the end of the eighteenth century a group of Belfast intellectuals feared the tradition was dying and the music would be lost. The festival gathered together ten harpers, mostly from the northern half of the island, and resulted in the publication of Edward Bunting's *Ancient Irish Music* in 1797, the first written record of traditional Irish harp music. A few years later the harp was a key symbol employed by the United Irishmen, although it was also used by the government militia which opposed the movement. The oldest surviving harp in Ireland is the fourteenth-century 'Brian Boru' harp in Trinity College Dublin, which has served as the model for depictions of the instrument on Irish coinage.

See also United Irishmen

Hockey

It is rare that a sport's introduction into Ireland can be pinned down with any precision, but with the game of hockey it is generally accepted that the year 1892 marked its first appearance on these shores. Hockey was introduced to Ireland by a Dublin schoolmaster, W.E. Paterson, who formed the first of half a dozen clubs that sprang up quickly within the following few years. The Irish Hockey Union was created in 1893. The origins of hockey are somewhat unclear – it has elements of hurling, shinty, lacrosse and football – but it is generally believed that it was named after the playing stick, which was called a hookey

H

because of its hooked appearance. Hockey differs from hurling in that it is a game based on ground-level play, and has only eleven players. The hockey ball is much heavier than the ball used in hurling, which is more often in the air than on the ground. However, when hockey was first introduced to Ireland, the players used hurleys for a short period before gradually adopting the regulation hockey sticks. The game tended to flourish most in the eastern half of Ireland, although it was also a popular game in Limerick and other parts of Munster. In Ulster enthusiasm for the game led to the formation of the Ulster Hockey Union in 1896, although this later became the Ulster branch of the Irish Hockey Union. Among the earliest northern clubs were Antrim, Ards, Banbridge, Cliftonville, Lisburn, North Down and Ulster, and some of the big firms in Belfast, such as Guinness, Imperial Tobacco, Short and Harland and the Albert Foundry, also had their own hockey clubs. The first main competition introduced was the Irish Senior Cup in 1894. Inter-provincial championships, dominated by Leinster and Ulster, followed in 1898. The first international hockey match ever played was a game between Ireland and Wales in 1894 (Ireland won 3–0), and in 1908, just sixteen years after the game was introduced to the country, Ireland were runners-up in the hockey competition at the Olympic Games.

See also Cricket, Hurling, Shinty

Holy Communion

Also known as the Eucharist, this is the central sacrament of Christian churches which was inspired by the actions of Jesus at the Last Supper. Drawn from the Greek word *eukharistia*, meaning 'thanksgiving', the Eucharist involves the partaking of consecrated bread and wine by the congregation. Within the Protestant churches, the bread

and wine are seen as symbolic of Christ's body and blood, but in the Catholic church it is believed that Christ is really and truly present in the consecrated bread and wine. Both Protestants and Catholics affirm the 'real presence' of Christ in the Eucharist; the differences lie in how this is interpreted or defined. The celebration of the Eucharist takes place daily in Catholic churches, and it is celebrated at least once a week within the Church of Ireland. In the Presbyterian church, Holy Communion is celebrated on average around six times per year, although within some churches it may be celebrated as rarely as twice a year. Methodist churches, which often refer to Communion as the Sacrament of the Lord's Supper, usually celebrate Holy Communion monthly.

See also Catechism, Catholic Church, Church of Ireland, Communion Tokens, Confirmation, Corpus Christi, First Communion, Mass, Methodist Church, Presbyterian Church

Holy Water

Special water which is blessed and used as a symbolic reminder of baptism within the Catholic church. Holy water fonts are usually found near the door of Catholic churches and members of the congregation will often use it to make the Sign of the Cross as they enter. Holy water is sometimes sprinkled as part of prayers of blessing, such as at funerals, over someone who is ill, or at the blessing of a house.

Home Rule

With the introduction of the Act of Union in 1801, the Irish parliament was abolished and Ireland was ruled from Westminster. Among those who opposed this state of affairs some, such as the Young Irelanders and the Fenians, saw violent uprising as the only means of obtaining self-determination, while others believed that constitutional methods offered the best hope of obtaining a domestic parliament and the repeal of the act which allowed Britain to govern Ireland. The first signs that constitutional pressure might force a change came in the 1870s, when Irish MPs standing as supporters of home rule began to be returned to the parliament at Westminster. Following the general election of 1886 the Irish Parliamentary Party, led by Charles Stewart Parnell, held the balance of power between the Liberals and the Conservatives. The Liberal leader, William Gladstone, became a convert to the cause of home rule and promised his support if Parnell backed the Liberals. The prospect of the union being broken prompted the creation of the first unionist movement, and Gladstone's bill to enact his promise was defeated when unionist members of his own party refused to support it. A second Home Rule Bill was introduced in 1893 but was defeated in the House of Lords. After the general election of 1910, the Irish MPs, now under the leadership of John Redmond, once again held the balance of power. A third Home Rule Bill was introduced by the Liberals in 1912. Unionist opposition to the bill, mobilised under the leadership of Sir Edward Carson, included mass signings of a Solemn League and Covenant and the formation of the Ulster Volunteer Force in 1913. The House of Lords once again defeated the bill, but parliamentary reform meant that their rejection could only be sustained for two years. In 1914, however, the outbreak of World War I interrupted the bill's enactment, causing intense frustration among supporters of home rule in Ireland. Members of the Irish Volunteers, which had been formed in 1913 to galvanise support for legislative independence, became split over the movement's direction. The majority of the Volunteers heeded Redmond's call to fight in the war, hoping that home rule would be introduced as an act of gratitude when hostilities ended. Others believed that home rule would never be granted, and in any case it did no go far enough, only giving Ireland dominion status within the British Empire rather than full independence. They planned to gain self-determination by violent means and so the seeds were sown for the 1916 Easter Rising, the subsequent rise of the IRA and the 1919–21 War of Independence. After the general election of 1918, in which Sinn Féin eclipsed the Irish Parliamentary Party, and

H

unionists held sway in the north-east of Ireland, the new government under David Lloyd-George decided that the only way to placate the increasingly polarised country was to set up separate parliaments north and south. Thus the scene was set for the Government of Ireland Act in 1920, and ultimately the partition of Ireland.

See also Act of Union, Easter Rising, Fenians, Gaelic League, Murals, Nationalism, Partition, Republicanism, Solemn League and Covenant, Unionism

Huguenots

French Protestants who fled Europe in the late seventeenth century to escape religious persecution. An estimated ten thousand Huguenots arrived in Ireland around this time, although some of them had settled here much earlier, and many fought with William of Orange during his Irish campaign. In 1698 a colony of Huguenots led by Louis Crommelin was encouraged to settle in Lisburn, County Antrim, where they laid the foundations for the Irish linen industry. Other communities were established in Lurgan, Dundalk, Castleblayney, Cork, Wexford and Dublin.

See also Battle of the Boyne, Linen, Protestantism

Hunger Strikes

The refusal of prisoners in jail to eat food has been a long-standing method of non-violent protest to achieve a variety of aims. In the past hunger strikes have been used to support claims of wrongful imprisonment, to seek improved conditions or status within the jail, or to seek transfers to jails closer to home. The most widely known hunger strike of recent times was mounted by republican prisoners in the Maze prison in

H

69

1980–1. The strike was in support of demands for republican inmates to be treated as political prisoners (which would give them the right to wear civilian clothes), segregation from loyalist prisoners, and exemption from prison work. Ten men died during the strike, including Bobby Sands, who before his death was elected MP for the Westminster seat of Fermanagh–South Tyrone. Due largely to the intervention of prisoners' families and clergy, the strike ended after eight months and was followed by the granting of some of the prisoners' demands.

See also Murals, Republicanism

Hurling

Hurling is said to be one of the oldest field sports in the world, and tradition has it that the game has been played in Ireland since the time of Cú Chulainn. Today hurling is most popular in those parts of Ireland roughly south of a line drawn from Dublin to Galway. In Ulster the game enjoys its greatest support in the Glens of Antrim and the Ards peninsula, leading some commentators to suggest that this is in part due to the historic ties between these two regions and the west coast of Scotland, where a similar game called shinty is a popular sport. Hurling is played on the same size of pitch and with the same number of players (fifteen) as Gaelic football, and the two main components of the game are the hurley, or *camán*, and the ball, or *sliotar*. The hurley is four feet long and has a flattened end, known as a 'boss', which must be no more than four

H

70

inches wide. The goalposts are the same as those used in Gaelic football, except that in the early days a goal (formerly worth five points) was scored by hitting the ball *over* the crossbar, and a point was scored by hitting the ball *under* the bar. This has now been changed to conform with Gaelic football, where a goal is scored underneath the crossbar and is worth three points. Annual challenge games between hurlers and shinty players take place in Ireland and Scotland on alternate years, with the players adopting the rules of the host country on each occasion.

See also Cricket, Gaelic Athletic Association, Hockey, Shinty

H

Independent Orange Order

A breakaway group from the Orange Order founded in 1903. The Independent Orange Order was formed by Lindsay Crawford, editor of the *Irish Protestant*, and Tom Sloan, leader of the Belfast Protestant Association, following Sloan's suspension from the Orange Order for heckling the Belfast County Grand Master on the Twelfth of July platform in 1902. Initially, the Independent Order's support for the labour movement and staunch anti-Catholicism won significant support among working-class Protestants, leading to the creation of fifty-five lodges, almost half of which were in Belfast. However, the influence of the Independent Order declined during the home rule crisis and today the order survives mainly in north Antrim.

See also Knights of Malta, Orange Order

Internment

The modern concept of detention without trial was first employed in Ireland in the turbulent years leading up to the Anglo-Irish Treaty in 1921. The future modernising *taoiseach*, Sean Lemass, was interned at Ballykinlar, County Down, in 1921, and the founder of Fianna Fáil, Eamon de Valera, was interned in England in 1918. As *taoiseach*, de Valera later ordered the internment of more than one thousand members of the IRA in the Irish Free State during World War II. During the violence that followed partition, internment was introduced in the North and in the South as a result of the murder of an MP in 1922 and again in response to a spate of IRA activity in 1942. Internment continued sporadically in the North until 1961, and was not reintroduced again until 9 August 1971, when the detention of some 240 men suspected of republican sympathies resulted in widespread protests and shootings. No loyalists were interned. In the violence that followed came the killing of the first Catholic priest and the first Ulster Defence Regiment soldier of the Troubles. A number of loyalists were later interned in 1973. The introduction of internment in 1971 had the marked effect of alienating nationalists generally, of increasing support for militant republicanism and of heightening antagonism towards the presence of the British army in Northern Ireland. Although detention without trial was abandoned in 1975, it scarred the nationalist and republican psyche and has been marked annually by demonstrations and occasionally riots.

See also Partition

Irish Language

Irish is a Celtic language (the Irish word for the language is *Gaeilge*) brought to Ireland by the expansion of the Celts westward across Europe in the first millennium BC. While the Celtic languages on the Continent were gradually overwhelmed by the spread of Latin, in Ireland, which was never conquered by the Roman Empire, the language of the Celts continued to flourish. Two distinct groups of languages were introduced by the Celts: within what is known as the P Group are the Welsh, Cornish and Breton tongues, while those in the Q Group include Irish, Scots and Manx. Modern-day Scots Gaelic is the result of the Irish language being introduced to Scotland from Ireland around AD 300 and up until the middle of the eighteenth century Scots Gaelic was actually called Irish. Standardisation of the Irish language began as early as the eighth century, long before attempts were made to regularise English, and there were a number of revisions of the grammatical forms in the centuries that followed. Consequently, modern Irish is as different from early Irish as current-day English is from Anglo-Saxon. The slow decline of the Irish language in the eastern half of Ireland began initially with the arrival of the Normans in the twelfth century, who brought French and English to these shores. French did not survive, but English

I

gained a foothold in the Pale around Dublin and spread inexorably outward. The seventeenth century plantation further encouraged the spread of English in the North, although paradoxically some of the planters were native Scots Gaelic speakers. Nevertheless, Irish continued to be spoken by significant numbers. Some 15 per cent of people born in Ulster in the first decade of the nineteenth century were native Irish speakers, and by the end of the century there were still native speakers to be found in every Ulster county. Most modern-day speakers in Northern Ireland have either learned Irish as a second language or are the children of people who learned Irish as a second language. The 1991 census revealed that there are 142,000 people (9.6 per cent of the Northern Ireland population) who claim to have a knowledge of the Irish language and considerable efforts are being made to foster a new generation of Irish speakers. The first Irish-speaking primary school in the North opened in 1971 and there are currently fourteen primary schools, two secondary schools and numerous playgroups where pupils are taught in Irish.

See also Celts, Fáinne, Gael,
Gaelic League, Gaeltacht,
Glór na nGael, Placenames

Irish National Foresters

The Irish National Foresters (INF) was one of a number of friendly societies which grew up in Ireland during the eighteenth and nineteenth centuries to provide health care, sickness pay and a variety of other welfare benefits to its members. The Foresters developed out of the Ancient Order of Foresters, an English organisation whose first Irish branch was established in Cork city in 1848. The INF broke away from the Ancient Order during a period of increasing nationalist awareness in Ireland and the first branch was formed in Dublin in 1877. Despite its surface nationalism (shamrocks, harps and Celtic

I

imagery were widely employed on INF banners) the Foresters were primarily a welfare organisation, providing free medical services and burial expenses for paid-up members, and their meetings were often social occasions. However, in common with many other friendly societies, the welfare aspect became redundant and the organisation went into decline with the passing of the 1911 Insurance Act, which ushered in statutory responsibilities for social care. Although the INF was at one time the largest friendly society in Ireland, with some 9,340 members and 128 branches, it is now a much smaller organisation and is almost exclusively devoted to organising social events and entertainment. The Ancient Order of Foresters, meanwhile, still survives; one branch of the organisation exists in Belfast.

See also Banner, Nationalism

I

Jews

Many Jewish families settled in Northern Ireland, and particularly in Belfast, during the last 150 years because of persecution elsewhere in Europe. Some fled the anti-Jewish pogroms in Lithuania at the turn of the century, while others came from countries occupied by the Nazis during World War II. A German linen merchant, Daniel Jaffe, is generally credited with founding the Belfast Jewish community, for he provided the funds for the city's first synagogue in 1864. His son, Sir Otto Jaffe, was elected lord mayor of the city on two occasions. Many members of the Jewish community have played an important role in the business and cultural life of the North through their involvement in medicine, the legal profession, manufacturing and the arts. Chaim Herzog, president of Israel 1983–93, was born in north Belfast in 1918. In 1960 it was estimated that there were some 1,500 Jews living in Belfast, but thirty years later there were no more than 200. The decline of the Jews in Belfast has been blamed chiefly on an ageing population, inter-faith marriages and emigration.

Jig

One of the few traditional dance metres which actually has its origins in Ireland, although the word itself appears to come from the Italian language. The jig is said to date back many centuries and some tunes are based on old clan marches, although most of those performed today were composed by pipers and fiddlers in the eighteenth and nineteenth centuries. The majority of Irish jigs are native in origin, and while some have been imported from England, very few have come from Scotland. There are three types of jig, all with different time signatures. The double jig, which is probably the most popular form, is played in six–eight time, the single jig is played in twelve–eight time and the slip or hop jig is played in nine–eight time.

See also Reel

J

Kirk Session

The kirk session is the governing body of a local Presbyterian church congregation, the members of which are elected and ordained to serve on the session for life. The minister of the congregation is the moderator, or chairman, of the kirk session. Operating in tandem with the kirk session is the congregational committee, which has responsibility for financial and property matters and whose members are elected regularly.

See also Presbyterian Church, Presbytery

Knights of Malta

There are a number of organisations in Ireland to which the term 'Knights of Malta' can be applied. The phrase has its origins in the crusades of the twelfth century, when a group of knights were charged with the protection of a Christian church and hospital dedicated to Saint John the Baptist and established in Jerusalem. After the recapture of Jerusalem by Islamic armies, the knights eventually found a new home on the island of Malta. They remained there for over five hundred years before being expelled by Napoleon in 1798 and it was not until 1834 that the order was reconstituted, primarily as an organisation to aid the sick. Knights of the Sovereign Order of Malta had been in Ireland many centuries prior to this period but were driven out by Henry VIII in 1540, and the order was only re-established in 1933. In keeping with its long tradition, the order retains a voluntary ambulance corps, but there is also a scale of knighthood degrees which ranges from Knights and Dames of Magistral Grace, a degree open to any practising Catholic, to Knights of Justice, the order's most senior degree, whose members must take vows of poverty, chastity and obedience. This particular Order of Malta is unique in that it is regarded as a

77

sovereign state which operates its own embassies in many countries, although like the Vatican, the organisation's actual territory is limited to its headquarters in Rome. Parallel to the Sovereign Order of Malta is the Venerable Order of Saint John, which looks back to the same chivalric tradition and was formed in England in 1831. The Venerable Order of Saint John has the appearance of being more secular, although it has a special relationship with the Anglican church. It also has a structure of knights and dames, membership of which is conferred as an honour by the British monarch. The Saint John Ambulance Association is maintained by the Venerable Order. Within freemasonry there are a series of 'Knights Templar' degrees inspired by the defence of Jerusalem at the time of the crusades and one of these degrees is known as the Knights of Malta. In Scotland there was an order of the Knights of Malta in the eighteenth century which claimed an origin in the historic pre-Reformation Sovereign Order of Malta. This order of knights is very similar in form to the Royal Black Institution and nowadays it stands in the same kind of relationship to the Independent Orange Order as the Black Institution does to the Orange Order.

Knights of Saint Columbanus

A Catholic fraternal society which has its origins in a laymen's religious organisation set up by a Belfast priest, Father James O'Neill, in the period around World War I. Its aim was to promote Catholic faith and education and within a short space of time the group's influence had spread throughout the North and also to Dublin. In 1922 this society was amalgamated with a similar organisation called the Columban Knights and the Knights of Saint Columbanus was officially formed. Many of the rituals practised by members were derived from a similar Catholic fraternity in the United States, the Knights of Saint Columbus, but a large proportion of them are no longer used.

See also Freemasons,
Independent Orange Order,
Royal Black Institution

K

Lambeg Drum

Tradition has it that this cylindrical drum, three foot in diameter and made from goatskin stretched over an oak frame, was first introduced to Ireland by William of Orange's soldiers in the late seventeenth century, but the first recorded use of the drum at Twelfth of July processions was not until a century later. As well as featuring at Orange parades, Lambegs have also been played at impromptu rural drumming endurance competitions, known as 'stick-ins', and on occasions in the past they have been heard at parades organised by the Ancient Order of Hibernians. Created by individual craftsmen, the drums may vary in size and weight and the method of construction

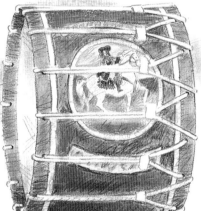 involves many time-consuming and often secret processes, with the goatskin being pared down to a parchment-like thickness to help to give the drum its characteristic high-pitched ringing sound. Until the late nineteenth century, Lambegs were played with wooden sticks, but nowadays they are usually beaten with twenty-two-inch malacca canes, which allow for an increased speed of playing and a volume of sound reaching 120 decibels – the threshold of pain for the human ear. The drums are also usually christened with individual names, such as Roaring Meg, the Pride of Down, or the Smasher, so called because of the number of times the skins were torn by over-enthusiastic drummers.

See also Ancient Order of Hibernians, Twelfth of July

Lammas Fair

Although now closely associated with the town of Ballycastle, County Antrim, mainly as a result of the popular song, 'The Oul' Lammas Fair', Lammas fairs were held in many towns across the land. They were originally held to mark the festival of *Lughnasa*, celebrating the first fruits of the harvest. The Lammas Fair in Ballycastle is held at the end of August, and the most famous items on sale are edible seaweed called 'dulse' and sticky toffee known as 'yellow man'.

See also Lughnasa

Linen

Flax, the plant which yields the fibres to make linen, has been grown in Ireland for around three hundred years, but it was not until the early eighteenth century that it became the source of a considerable manufacturing industry. Although flax was grown all over Ireland, it was in the North that the industry flourished, nurtured initially by Huguenot settlers in counties Armagh, Antrim and Down. Many farmers grew it on their land to supplement their incomes, but it was a highly labour-intensive process. The flax had to be pulled out of the ground by hand, dragged through a large iron comb to remove the seed, and then placed in a lint-hole full of stagnant water for around a fortnight to rot the central woody part of the stalk. Anything up to another fortnight was spent drying the flax, and then it would be scutched by crushing the flax so that the usable part could be more easily removed from the unusable part. The fibres would be spun into yarn in a mill and the yarn would be woven into cloth in a factory. In the early days of linen production it was very much a cottage industry, but with the coming of the Industrial Revolution and the introduction of modern production methods imported from the cotton mills of England, linen became the most important industry in Ulster. At its peak, during the years surrounding World

L

War I, almost 38,000 power looms were weaving linen in Ireland –
all but 3,000 of them in the North. A majority of the employees in
the linen industry were women, although the senior managerial
positions were invariably held by men. Despite strong demand for
linen during World War II and the years immediately afterwards,
production declined sharply in the 1950s and 1960s with the
introduction of man-made fibres. Today, only a handful of mills and
factories survive.

See also Huguenots, Quakers

Loyalism

A political and social ethos
which has traditionally combined unionism, strong monarchist
beliefs, Protestantism and support for the state of Northern Ireland
(usually referred to by loyalists as 'Ulster'). Loyalism has often been
painted as simply a more extreme form of unionism and while there
are certainly elements of this, there is a much more complex
relationship between the two, as well as many subtle but significant
differences. Perhaps one of the most important differences is
connected with social class; unionism has tended to be a more
middle- and upper-class phenomenon, while loyalism is more
deeply rooted in the working class. Where unionism is a credo based
upon political argument, loyalism is more of a belief based on faith,
upbringing, environment and community
identity. Religious affiliation is a key factor
within loyalism; it is possible to be a
Catholic unionist but not a Catholic
loyalist. Unionism places its strongest
emphasis on the link between
Britain and Northern Ireland
and will normally tend to take
a more broad view of the
relationships between the North
and its neighbours, while loyalism is
perceived to be more inward-looking with a greater emphasis on
self-reliance, its own historical icons, and the need to vigorously
defend the sovereignty of Ulster. This last principle has led to the

L

founding of a number of loyalist paramilitary organisations and also
to the staging of protests such as the Ulster Workers' Council strike
of 1974, carried out in opposition to the power-sharing Executive.
Modern unionists tend to use political means, such as rallies, non-
co-operation or even politicians resigning their seats, to make
known their opposition to a particular issue, while loyalists will
often employ more direct methods of protest and in many cases
resort to violence.

See also Battle of the Somme,
Nationalism, Protestantism,
Republicanism, Titanic, Ulster,
Unionism

Lughnasa

A pre-Christian festival
named after the Celtic god Lugh which marked the beginning of
the harvest. Celtic mythology has it that Lugh was given the secret
of the best days to sow the land and reap the harvest by an enemy
he vanquished in battle. *Lughnasa* was held at the beginning of
August and the modern Irish language word for that month is
Lúnasa. Many placenames across the Celtic world owe their origins
to Lugh, such as Louth, London and Lyon.

See also Bealtaine, Celts,
Lammas Fair, Samhain

Lundy

Lieutenant Colonel Robert
Lundy was the military governor of the city of Derry at the
beginning of the siege in April 1689, and his name has become
synonymous with a fear and resentment of betrayal within loyalism.
At the commencement of the siege Lundy adopted a defeatist
attitude and a number of military blunders led others in the city to
believe that the governor was less than wholehearted in his
resistance to the Jacobite forces outside the walls. When Lundy
refused the support of two army regiments sent from Liverpool, a
citizens' revolt led by Adam Murray removed him from power, and

L

he was replaced by Major Henry Baker and the Reverend George Walker. The new joint governors allowed Lundy to flee the besieged city disguised as a common soldier. One hundred years later the first recorded burning of an effigy of Lundy took place at events commemorating the centenary of the siege. Thus began a tradition of consigning to the bonfire effigies and emblems representing those accused of betraying Protestant Ulster.

See also Apprentice Boys of Derry, Siege of Derry

L

Mass

A Catholic name for the celebration of the Eucharist (Holy Communion). The term is generally believed to be derived from the words spoken at the end of the Latin version of the service, '*Ite, missa est* – 'Go, the congregation is dismissed'.

See also Catholic Church, Holy Communion

Meeting House

Formerly, a Presbyterian house of worship was called a meeting house. It was simple in style with largely functional decor, although the windows were usually ornamented with stained glass. Often the interior of the meeting house included a balcony around three sides of the building. Today the term meeting house is more usually applied to a Quaker house of worship, where there are no elaborate furnishings such as stained glass, memorials, pulpit or altar.

See also Presbyterian Church, Quakers

Methodist Church

Two distinguishing features of the Methodist church in Ireland are its special emphasis on preaching and its strong sense of social conscience – traditions which were close to the heart of the church's founding father, John Wesley. Ordained as an Anglican priest, Wesley became disenchanted with the Church of England's elitism in the eighteenth century and on 24 May 1738 he underwent a powerful spiritual experience which inspired him to create a new church based on the guiding principles of a small evangelical society at Oxford dubbed the 'Methodists', of which Wesley was a member. Over a period of more than forty years Wesley made twenty-one visits to Ireland, the first on 9 August 1747. Wesley's enthusiasm for lively preaching took him all over the country, but it also brought him into conflict with the Established Church. In some quarters Methodists were regarded

M

almost as fanatics and on occasions the preachers were attacked by mobs. Allied to their evangelical message was a campaigning zeal for improving living conditions for the working classes, and as a result Methodism tended to thrive in deprived city areas and poverty-ridden parts of the country. Schools and orphanages were established to help the underprivileged. This social awareness is continued in the modern Methodist church, particularly through its Council on Social Responsibility, which addresses contemporary ethical issues in Ireland and around the world. The long-standing tradition of preaching is maintained through its special place in weekly church services – as much as one-third of the service may be devoted to preaching – and also through the large number of lay preachers within Methodism, some of whom will conduct entire Sunday services. The structure of the Methodist church in Ireland is similar in many ways to that of the Presbyterian church. Local churches are administered by a leaders' meeting, which consists of the minister and lay people. Churchgoers are represented at these meetings by one congregational representative for every fifty members. Ministers and laity from churches in a circuit will gather for quarterly meetings, and circuit representatives will meet twice a year at district synods. The supreme body within the church is the Annual Conference, which elects a president each year. According to the 1991 census, there were just under 60,000 Methodists in Northern Ireland, making it the fourth largest denomination.

See also Circuit, Confirmation, Evangelism, Holy Communion, Methodist Conference, Protestant, Synod

Methodist Conference

The Annual Conference of the Methodist church in Ireland is held in June, shortly before the beginning of the church's year on 1 July. The conference is attended by ministers and lay representatives from each of the 125 circuits in Ireland and one of its chief tasks is to elect a president (the Methodist equivalent of a Presbyterian moderator). The minister appointed to the task is designated at the previous Annual Conference and does

M

not take up the post until his official appointment the following year. The president serves a one-year term and is normally elected to the role only once during his life time. Like the Presbyterian moderator, the role of the Methodist president is more representative than executive.

See also Circuit, Methodist Church, Moderator

Missal

A prayer book used by members of the Catholic faith which contains prayers, readings and so forth of the Masses for a complete year.

See also Holy Communion, Mass

Moderator

The moderator is the senior representative of the Presbyterian church in Ireland, and unlike the leaders of the episcopal churches, he (or she – the Presbyterian church was the first to ordain women as ministers in Ireland) serves only a one-year term and usually occupies the position just once. The moderator is elected at the General Assembly of the Presbyterian church in Ireland in June each year. During a term of office, the moderator acts as a spokesperson for the church but in keeping with Presbyterianism's strict democratic code, he or she has no special executive powers. On the back of the moderator's chair are carved the words *primus inter pares*, 'first among equals'.

See also General Assembly, Presbyterian Church

Moravians

The Moravians, members of the Ancient Church of the Brethren, which has its roots in eastern Europe, became established in Ireland in the mid-eighteenth century. With German and Dutch help, the Moravians founded a model community run on strict religious principles at Gracehill, County Antrim, and at one time as many as five hundred Moravians lived there. By 1850, however, people who did not subscribe to the Moravian faith were also allowed to settle in the village. According to the 1991 census, there are some seven hundred active Moravians in Northern Ireland.

Mount Sandel

An archaeological site near Coleraine, County Londonderry, that contains the earliest evidence of human habitation anywhere in Ireland. Excavation at the site in the 1970s discovered the remains of igloo-shaped houses made from bent saplings and covered with animal hide which were constructed eight thousand years previously.

M

Mumming

Despite being associated with Christmas, one of the key dates in the Christian calendar, mumming is a tradition with pagan overtones that may possibly have been brought to Ireland in Norman times. The traditional time for mumming was the twelve days of Christmas, when mummers, dressed in straw masks and suits, would travel from house to house, into pubs and halls, playing pranks and causing merriment. One of the main features of Christmas mumming is the custom of visiting houses in disguise. Members of the troupe will try to hide their identity with odd clothes, straw and garments normally worn by the opposite sex, while the hosts who are being visited have to guess the identity of the person beneath the camouflage. Mummers also perform a traditional play, lasting around fifteen minutes, which involves a combat between two heroes and the eventual resurrection of the one who has been defeated. In Northern Ireland the mumming tradition remains strongest today in counties Armagh and Fermanagh.

Murals

A tradition dating back to the early part of the twentieth century, the first known examples of wall murals in the North depicted the familiar image of William of Orange and were painted in east Belfast during the years surrounding the home rule issue in 1912. It has been said that the tradition of murals evolved at this time because house paint was widely available for the first time, advertising billboards were becoming ever more present, and the painting of walls was a natural extension of the loyalist tradition of street decoration. Loyalist murals continued to be popular following the creation of Northern

Ireland in 1921, but there was a lull in activity during World War II and afterwards until the onset of the Troubles in 1969. Most republican murals date from this time onwards, although there are a few earlier examples. Probably the most famous example of wall-painting anywhere in the North is the 'Free Derry' wall, which was first painted in October 1968. The hunger strikes of 1980–1 sparked the most concerted period of republican mural painting, with perhaps upwards of 150 appearing at this time, and the parades controversy of the 1990s has once again led to an upsurge in wall-painting in nationalist areas. Within both traditions, murals are often found in working-class housing estates and are seen as a local expression of identity. Statutory agencies are generally unwilling to make any attempt to remove murals if they are made with the consent of the people living in the area, though on occasions some have been removed following complaints.

See also Home Rule, Hunger Strikes, Loyalism, Republicanism

M

National Anthem

The official patriotic song of any country is known as the national anthem. In Northern Ireland the words 'national anthem' are taken to refer to 'God Save the Queen', while 'The Soldier's Song', the national anthem of the Republic of Ireland, is usually referred to by its name. 'God Save the Queen' (the title and words of the song change gender according to the sex of the monarch) has been in use on public occasions since 1745, although its origins go back much further than that. It is not known who composed the melody or who penned the words. Official regulations for performance of the song in public were first drawn up in 1933.

See also The Soldier's Song

Nationalism

A political and cultural credo which aspires to a thirty-two-county Ireland under one government consisting of Irish men and women elected by the Irish people. Although Ireland did have its own parliament for over one hundred years until the Act of Union in 1801, it was an emasculated body representing the interests of landowners and subservient to the English parliament. Attempts to give the Irish some control over their own destiny, such as Henry Grattan's campaign for legislative independence in the 1780s, or the home rule campaigns of the late nineteenth and early twentieth centuries, concentrated on political empowerment and were not directed at removing British sovereignty over Ireland. These constitutional efforts to secure Irish self-determination took place alongside military campaigns waged by the United Irishmen, the Young Ireland movement, the Fenians and the Irish Republican Brotherhood (IRB), whose aims were to completely remove British authority in Ireland, and the two strands are representative of the central debate

N

at the heart of modern nationalism – whether or not the use of force is justified in the pursuit of Irish unification. Increasingly, nationalism has come to be identified with the constitutional pursuit of Irish unity while military efforts to achieve the same goal are usually associated with republicanism. Both ideologies, however, have many points of contact, such as a basic non-acceptance of the validity of the northern state and a belief that those with nationalist aspirations have been discriminated against in Northern Ireland. Culturally, nationalism has been identified with Catholicism since the formation of Daniel O'Connell's Catholic Association, and the Gaelic cultural revival at the end of the nineteenth century also brought language, sport, music, literature and Celtic folklore within the Irish nationalist vision. This is a view which is being challenged by some modernist nationalist thinkers who see their goal as the creation of a 'new Ireland' rather than one based upon traditional notions.

See also Act of Union, Catholic Church, Fenians, Gaelic League, Home Rule, Loyalism, Republicanism, Unionism, United Irishmen

Navan Fort

Dubbed Ulster's Camelot, Navan Fort is an Iron Age site outside Armagh city thought to be the seat of the high kings of Ulster. The ancient name for the site, Emain Macha (the twins of Macha), is derived from a story from the Ulster Cycle of Tales in which the heavily pregnant Macha gives birth to twins after being forced to run in a race against a chariot. Her birth pangs were so

N

severe that she cursed all those who heard her screams, condemning them to suffer similar pains for five days at the time of their greatest difficulty. Many other figures from the Ulster Cycle of Tales – Cú Chulainn, Conchobar, the Red Branch knights – also have strong associations with Emain Macha. Archaeological evidence shows that Navan Fort was occupied as early as 2000 BC, though its era of great importance appears to be around 700 BC. Significant finds at the site have included the Loughnashade Trumpet (now in the care of the National Museum in Dublin), the skull of a Barbary ape (which suggests that its inhabitants traded with the Mediterranean), and the largest dog skull found anywhere in the British Isles – an echo of the links with Cú Chulainn, the 'hound of Ulster'. It is believed that Saint Patrick established Armagh as the centre of Christianity in Ireland because of its proximity to Emain Macha.

See also Cú Chulainn, Deirdre of the Sorrows, Red Branch Knights, Ulster Cycle of Tales

Non-Subscribing Presbyterian Church

A church officially formed in Ireland in 1910 following a split within the Presbyterian church in the early nineteenth century over allegiance to the Westminster Confession of Faith, the church's central statement of belief. Every minister and elder within the mainstream Presbyterian church in Ireland must sign the Westminster Confession to be eligible to serve within the church. However, at the time of the split, a number of Presbyterians refused to sign and broke away from the Synod of Ulster because they preferred to take their teachings directly from the Bible rather than accept any 'man-made' authority. The dispute divided congregations and resulted in new churches being built in many towns. There are currently around 3,200 Non-Subscribing Presbyterians in Northern Ireland.

See also Presbyterian Church

N

Normans

The Normans may have invaded England in 1066, but when they arrived in Ireland a century later it was certainly not as an invasion force. The first Normans to land on Irish soil were invited here by the king of Leinster, Dermot MacMurrough, who sought their help in strengthening his hold over his kingdom. MacMurrough offered one of the most powerful knights, Richard de Clare, known more commonly by his nickname of Strongbow, the future kingship of Leinster in return for his help. When MacMurrough died the high king, Rory O'Connor, attempted to throw Strongbow out of Ireland. He failed ignominiously and the English king, Henry II, was forced to travel to Ireland with an army to quell any further ambitions Strongbow may have had. A year after Strongbow's death in 1176, another ambitious Norman, John de Courcy, embarked on a lightning conquest of eastern Ulster with a small but highly trained force of around three hundred men and twenty-two horsemen. Over a period of some twenty years his efforts to carve out a fiefdom for himself also met with royal disapproval and de Courcy was driven out by Hugh de Lacy, who was created earl of Ulster in 1205. Within a century, however, the Norman hold on Ireland was slackening as a result of warfare, famine, the Black Death and the assimilation of many Normans into Irish society. The legacy of the Normans remains highly visible today, in castles such as Carrickfergus, Dundrum and Carlingford, ecclesiastical settlements such as Inch Abbey and Grey Abbey, and in surnames such as FitzGerald, Butler, Savage, Logan

N

and Power. It was also the Normans who brought the English language and a new system of land division to Ireland.

See also County, Demesne, Irish Language, Parish, Placenames, Province, Ulster, Whiskey

Novena

A Catholic tradition which takes its name from the Latin word for nine. A novena is a series of prayers for a particular intention which usually lasts nine days but on some occasions may last nine weeks. The prayers may be said by an individual or they may be said by a congregation. At some parish-based novenas members of the congregation will write out the object of their prayers and these will be read out by the priest to elicit the support of all the worshippers. Notable novenas include the Novena to Our Lady of Perpetual Succour, the Novena to Our Lady of Lourdes, held in February, and a novena held for nine days in June leading to the Feast of the Sacred Heart. Often these prayer events will draw crowds of several thousands.

See also Catholic Church, Sacred Heart of Jesus

Nun

A term which is commonly used nowadays to refer to a member of any female Catholic or Anglican religious order who has taken vows of poverty, chastity and obedience. Strictly speaking, however, the word refers to a female member of a closed religious order where outsiders are not normally permitted to enter and those inside are rarely allowed to leave. In some instances a female member of a religious order who is engaged in work in the outside world is not a nun in the strict sense of the word but is more correctly known as a 'sister'.

See also Convent

N

Orange Lily

Although the wearing or display of orange lilies has been widely used in Ireland to denote allegiance to the Williamite cause, William III used the orange tree rather than the lily as a symbol of his leadership of the House of Orange. The use of orange lilies probably dates from around the mid-eighteenth century, but the peak of their popularity (they were often used on arches in Twelfth of July celebrations) was in the early to mid-nineteenth century. Orange lilies can often be found depicted on loyalist drums and banners.

See also Arch, Banner, Easter Lily, Twelfth of July

Orange Order

Founded after the party affray of the Battle of the Diamond at Loughgall, County Armagh, in September 1795, the Orange Order developed from a number of Protestant organisations which had been in existence previously, most notably the Orange Boys, created by James Wilson of Dyan, County Tyrone, in 1793. Thus when the Order was founded, according to tradition in a field near Dan Winter's cottage at Loughgall, Dyan was designated Lodge Number 1, and other Orange Boys clubs in existence at that time were given similarly early lodge numbers. By March 1798, the date of the formation of the Grand Lodge of Ireland, there were 470 lodges in existence throughout Ireland. As an organisation pledged to defend Protestantism and support the monarchy, the order continued to grow in numbers and influence throughout the British Isles. However, in 1835, following investigations by a parliamentary committee of inquiry, in which it was suggested that the Orange Order was a force for a potential coup d'état, William IV's brother, the Duke of Cumberland, who was Grand Master at the time,

O

dissolved the Grand Lodge of Great Britain at the king's request. The Grand Lodge of Ireland was also dissolved, and although local lodges continued to function, the parent body was not re-formed until 1846. The Grand Lodge elects its officers annually from the ranks of county lodge officers, who in turn are drawn from district lodges. Districts are groups of individual local lodges. To join a lodge, a candidate must be an adherent of one of the Protestant religions, and following a simple initiation ceremony, he is granted an Orange degree, usually followed six months later by another ritual which entitles him to a Plain Purple degree. He is then eligible to join the Royal Arch Purple Chapter, once he has gone through the ritual of the Royal Arch Purple degree. Although the phrase 'civil and religious liberty' is often associated with the Orange Order, these words cannot be found in the organisation's constitution, which is based upon defence of the sovereign, the upholding of Protestantism, the protection of Protestant lives and property and the rejection of all religious intolerance. There are currently around two thousand Orange lodges in Ireland, and approximately eighty thousand active members of the order. Orange institutions can also be found in most areas of the world which were formerly part of the British Empire, though membership in these countries is generally declining. The Grand Orange Council of the World was founded in 1867 and meets every three years in a different country.

See also Arch, Banner, Battle of the Boyne, Battle of the Diamond, Bowler Hat, Independent Orange Order, Orange Lily, Peep o' Day Boys, Protestantism, Royal Arch Purple, Royal Black Institution, Sash, Sham Fight, Twelfth of July

O

Parish

An area of land which is the smallest geographical unit of administration within the Catholic church and the Church of Ireland. Within the Catholic church, the clergyman in charge of the parish is the parish priest, while in the Church of Ireland the minister in charge is known as the rector or the vicar. The system of parishes was formalised in Ireland by the Normans in the twelfth century and after the Reformation the same boundaries were retained by the Church of Ireland. Over the years Catholic parish boundaries have often been redrawn to suit population shifts. The parish system was also used by the government as areas of civil administration, with a number of parishes making up the larger unit of a barony. Parishes tend to vary dramatically in size, with some containing as little as three townlands, while others are made up of more than two hundred townlands.

See also Barony, Priest, Rector, Townland

Partition

The division of Ireland into the six-county Northern Ireland and the twenty-six counties of Southern Ireland was enacted in the British parliament by the 1920 Government of Ireland Act. The legislation was applied to the North on 1 May 1921, but it never came into effect in the South. It was superseded by the Anglo-Irish Treaty six months later, which effectively defined the whole of Ireland as a self-governing unit with dominion status. However, the North was given the option of retaining its separate status under the Government of Ireland Act, which it duly exercised. Nationalists were totally opposed to the whole idea of partition, while some people who supported it were concerned that not all of the nine counties of the ancient province of Ulster were to be included in the new northern state. However, unionists felt that a nine-county Northern Ireland would not give them a sufficiently large majority in the new parliament and it was

P

feared that the state would be voted out of existence within a short time of being created.

See also Boundary Commission, Free State, Home Rule, Loyalism, Nationalism, Province, Republicanism, Stormont, Unionism

Peep o' Day Boys

A Protestant, mainly Presbyterian, faction that conducted night raids on Catholic homes in County Armagh during the open sectarian conflict that existed in the county from 1784 until 1796. Well-armed but poorly organised, the Peep o' Day Boys were divided into local groups known as fleets, such as the Bawn Fleet of Hamiltonsbawn and the Nappagh Fleet. So named because many of their attacks were carried out before dawn, or the 'peep o' day', the vigilantes claimed they were searching Catholic houses for illegal arms, but the attacks were so brutal and indiscriminate that many of the Protestant gentry lent guns to neighbouring Catholics so they could defend themselves. One of the first acts of the newly formed Orange Order in 1795 was to condemn the actions of the Peep o' Day Boys and disassociate itself from the vigilante group.

See also Battle of the Diamond, Defenders, Orange Order

Pioneer Total Abstinence Association

A temperance organisation within the Catholic church, founded in 1901. The association has its roots in a Catholic spiritual group known as the Apostleship of Prayer, which drew its inspiration from the Sacred Heart. The director of this group, James Cullen, founded a temperance branch of the organisation and called it the Total Abstinence League of the Sacred Heart. This

P

group encouraged people to renounce alcohol, and its most senior members, who had taken a lifelong commitment to sobriety, were known as Pioneers. The Pioneers were highly influential in encouraging temperance and today remain active campaigners against alcohol. Those who join the association and take the pledge of abstinence are awarded a Pioneer pin, a shield-shaped lapel badge with a depiction of the Sacred Heart.

See also Sacred Heart of Jesus

Placenames

The names of towns, villages, townlands and other geographical features in Northern Ireland are mostly English language versions of Irish language names, since the majority of people spoke Irish up until the seventeenth century. The familiar prefix 'bally' is a corruption of the Irish *baile*, meaning 'township', while *dún* means a 'fort', *ráth* refers to a 'ringfort', and *cill* means a 'church'. The influence of the Viking settlers on placenames is limited to Strangford and Carlingford loughs, the suffix 'ford' being derived from the Norse word *fjord*. The Norman legacy is more striking, however, with many placenames in eastern Ulster bearing their stamp. A surname followed by the word 'town' (from the old English *tun*, meaning 'settlement') is often an indication that the roots of that place are in Norman times. The wholesale arrival of planters from Scotland and England in the seventeenth century speeded up the anglicisation of many Irish placenames and also led to the introduction of many new names for towns and villages which developed as a result of the settlers' arrival.

See also Barony, County, Demesne, Irish Language, Normans, Parish, Province, Townland, Ulster, Vikings

Plantation

A strategy of planned colonisation of Ireland which began in the wake of the

P

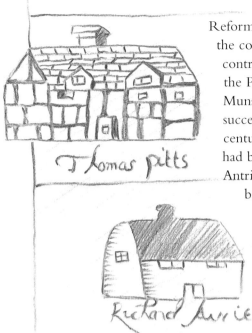

Thomas pitts

Richard Lawrie

Reformation in an attempt to bring the country under stronger English control. Efforts to plant settlers in the Pale around Dublin and in Munster had met with limited success in the late sixteenth century, and a number of settlers had become established in counties Antrim and Down by the beginning of the seventeenth century. But it was not until Hugh O'Neill had been defeated and left Ireland in the Flight of the Earls of 1607 that the plantation of Ulster began in earnest. The lands abandoned by the Gaelic lords were confiscated and given to Protestant English and Scottish 'undertakers' who promised to clear their lands entirely of the native Irish (something they failed to do) and bring more settlers to Ulster. The remaining Gaelic lords in Ulster made room for the new settlers in return for secure titles to their lands which were recognised by English law. As the planters streamed across Ulster, new towns and villages were established, typically with defensive walls, a diamond or market square and streets running at right angles to each other. The granting of lands in the north-west to London companies, who agreed to bring settlers, led to a change of name for the city of Derry to Londonderry and the county of Coleraine was also renamed Londonderry. By 1622 there were around thirteen thousand planters in Ulster, but the settlers were still vastly outnumbered by the native Irish, among whom high land rents and planter antagonism towards their Catholicism was causing growing resentment that would eventually spill over into the rebellion of 1641.

See also Bawn, Flight of the Earls, Placenames, Rebellion of 1641

P

100

Point-to-Point

A cross-country horse race which takes place on natural land rather than over a specially laid-out course. The first recorded point-to-point race in Ireland was held between two gentlemen racing over four miles of farmland in County Cork in 1752, though it is certain that the practice of point-to-point racing was a common occurrence throughout the country much earlier than this. All the features of a normal racecourse, including officials and bookmakers, are usually present at a point-to-point, although everything is more informal and on a much smaller scale. Steeplechase jockeys in Ireland will often begin their careers on the point-to-point circuit.

Potato

One of the staples of the Irish diet, potatoes have been grown in the North for four hundred years, and are the main ingredient of many well-known local dishes such as champ and potato bread. Some poteen-makers also use potatoes as the basic ingredient for their illicit whiskey. The potato was allegedly introduced to Ireland after samples of the crop were found aboard a wrecked ship of the Spanish Armada in the 1580s, but it was not until the eighteenth century that it became a commonly used foodstuff. Eventual over-reliance on the crop for food led to disaster in 1845 when potato blight, a fungus which promoted rotting, ruined much of the crop in Ireland and the result was a widespread famine. The early cultivation of potatoes was a labour-intensive process involving the manual digging of fields with spades, hand-sowing the seed from a 'guggerin' bag, and the enlisting of young and old to help harvest the crop. Mechanisation began with the patenting of the first mechanical potato digger by J. Hanson of Doagh, County Antrim, in 1852 and

P

later with the introduction of tractors during World War I. However, even as late as the 1940s, some farmers would still have dug their potato fields by hand and today people of all ages are regularly called on to help with the harvest. In many rural schools pupils are given unofficial time off classes to help with the potato picking. Despite the continued popularity of the vegetable, the amount of farmland given over to potato cultivation in Northern Ireland in 1997 was just 10 per cent of what it was in 1947.

See also Champ, Famine, Potato Bread, Poteen

Poteen

For as long as governments have attempted to control by licence the production of whiskey in Ireland, there have been illicit distillers operating in remote parts of the countryside. Poteen is the anglicised form of *poitín*, an Irish language word meaning 'small pot', which refers to the container the illegal spirit was usually made in. Many enterprising inhabitants of the more inaccessible parts of Ireland turned to making poteen in the seventeenth and eighteenth centuries when crippling taxes forced up the price of legally produced whiskey. In the early nineteenth century it was estimated that one-third of all the whiskey drunk in Ireland was distilled illegally, and the subsequent loss to the exchequer prompted the government to mount a strenuous campaign to stamp out the practice. The bitter battle of wits which ensued between the poteen-makers and the revenue men became the source of many songs and stories. The spirit continues to be made today, albeit on a much smaller scale, with recipes and quality varying dramatically from producer to producer. A recent estimate has put the number of illegal stills currently operating in Northern Ireland at 250.

P

Presbyterian Church

The church of state in Scotland, the Church of Scotland, is Presbyterian, as opposed to the Established Church in England, which is Anglican. At the time of the early-seventeenth-century plantation of Ulster, Presbyterianism was brought to north-east Ireland by the lowland Scots who travelled across the North Channel to their new home. The organised Presbyterian church in Ulster was established by Scottish Covenanters who landed here with the army of Major General Robert Monro during the rebellion of the 1640s and the first presbytery was created at Carrickfergus, County Antrim, on 10 June 1642. Presbyterian numbers grew quickly, reaching an estimated 217,000 by 1659. Thirty years later Ulster Presbyterian ministers formed themselves into the Synod of Ulster, which was the first dissenting synod in the British Isles (the Ulster Presbyterians 'dissented' against the Established Church of Ireland, while in Scotland their church *was* the Established Church). The dissenting Presbyterians were excluded from most public offices by an act of 1704 which required all government post-holders to receive Anglican communion at least once a year, and Presbyterian marriages did not achieve full legal recognition in Ireland until 1845. In 1836 the Synod of Ulster reinforced the requirement that its ministers subscribe unequivocally to the 1645 Westminster Confession of Faith, the official statement of Presbyterian doctrine, but this led to a split within the church and ultimately to the formation of the Non-Subscribing Presbyterian church. At this time (1840) the Synod of Ulster united with the Secession Synod (formed as a result of an earlier split in Scotland) to form the

P

General Assembly of the Presbyterian church in Ireland. It was also around this time that Presbyterian numbers in Ireland reached their highest ever level, with a total of 642,000 church members. Today, with some 337,000 members, the Presbyterian church remains the second largest church in Northern Ireland (in terms of Ireland as a whole, it is the third largest behind the Catholic church and the Church of Ireland). The Presbyterian church prides itself on its democratic system of accountability and checks and balances, and Presbyterians remain deeply suspicious of centralised power within the church. It is claimed that Presbyterian principles substantially influenced the drawing up of the constitution of the United States of America.

See also Burning Bush, Communion Tokens, Confirmation, Free Presbyterian Church of Ulster, General Assembly, Holy Communion, Kirk Session, Meeting House, Moderator, Non-Subscribing Presbyterian Church, Presbytery, Protestantism, Rebellion of 1641, Ruling Elder, Synod

Presbytery

In the Presbyterian church, a presbytery is a decision-making body made up of an equal number of ministers and elders appointed by the kirk sessions of the congregations within a particular locality. Several presbyteries are grouped into a synod. Within the Catholic faith, the home of a parish priest, usually known as a parochial house, may also be called a presbytery.

See also Kirk Session, Presbyterian Church, Ruling Elder, Synod

Priest

An ordained clergyman with the authority to administer the sacraments of the church. In the Catholic tradition, with which the term is most closely associated, the parish priest is a senior priest appointed to the spiritual care of a parish. In the Church of Ireland a minister is ordained as a priest,

P

but when in charge of a parish is more likely to be known as a rector or a vicar.

See also Catholic Church, Church of Ireland, Curate, Parish, Rector

Protestant

Protestantism is not a religion, nor is there any such thing as the Protestant church, although in past times the word Protestant was often used to describe a member of the Church of Ireland. Protestantism in the modern sense is a loose term defining those who do not accept papal authority over the Christian church and belong to churches that were separated from Roman communion during the Reformation of the sixteenth century. The doctrinal differences between the various churches under the broad umbrella of Protestantism are and have been very considerable. Perhaps one of the few common themes of Protestantism in Ireland is that it stresses the importance of the individual's private relationship with God.

See also Baptist Church, Brethren, Catholic Church, Church of Ireland, Free Presbyterian Church, Methodist Church, Non-Subscribing Presbyterian Church, Presbyterian Church, Quakers

Province

The four provinces of Ireland are based on ancient kingdoms. The Irish word for province is *cúige*, which means a 'fifth', since there were originally five provinces – Ulster, Munster, Leinster, Connacht and Meath. This system of land division was initially retained by the English in their attempts to define Irish land boundaries in the centuries following the arrival of the Normans. Meath was absorbed into the province of Leinster in the seventeenth century.

P

See also Ulster

Quakers

The first Quakers came to Ireland from England around the year 1650, and within two centuries they formed a thriving and industrious community which played an active part in the development of the linen industry, the railways and steamship companies. Also known as the Society of Friends, the Quakers were founded by a group of individual Puritan congregations under the leadership of George Fox in the aftermath of the English Civil War (1642–5). Often persecuted in Ireland for their neutrality in both the Williamite Wars and the rebellion of 1798, Quakers were also imprisoned for their refusal to pay church tithes. Their strong humanitarian beliefs led them to make a substantial, and all too often forgotten, contribution to famine relief in the mid-nineteenth century. The Quakers were also at the forefront of temperance, anti-slavery and prison reform campaigns. Bessbrook in County Armagh is a distinctive example of a model village created by the Quakers.

See also Famine, Linen

Q

Rebellion of 1641

The success of the plantation of Ulster in the early years of the seventeenth century had left Gaelic lords and the native Irish either dispossessed or severely disadvantaged, and they determined to win back their lands and rapidly disappearing lifestyle in a rebellion planned for 23 October 1641. However, on the night before the rising, government officials in Dublin received information about the plot and made swift arrests. The rebellion was effectively subdued in most of Ireland, but in Ulster it went ahead as planned. Initially it was highly effective and well co-ordinated, but as more and more of the peasantry joined the rebellion the Gaelic lords began to lose control. A number of massacres of planters took place and captives were often allowed to die of exposure and starvation. The extent of the killings is the subject of much dispute, ranging from wild estimates of 150,000 (there were nowhere near that many Protestants living in Ulster at the time) to a more conservative guess of 12,000, although even this may be excessive. Similar brutality was visited on the native Irish when the Scots army of Major General Robert Monro arrived in Ulster in 1642 to aid the settlers, but four years later he received a crushing defeat at the hands of Owen Roe O'Neill's army at the Battle of Benburb. Continuing unrest and faction fighting brought Oliver Cromwell to Ireland in 1649 and he ruthlessly destroyed all opposition.

See also Battle of the Boyne,
Plantation, Presbyterian Church

Rebellion of 1798

An uprising led by the United Irishmen which attempted to overthrow English authority in Ireland but ultimately failed because of informers, poor communications and organisation, key arrests by government forces and the failure of substantial foreign aid to materialise. Eighteen months before the beginning of the insurrection, a planned invasion by the French fleet at Bantry Bay in County Cork had been aborted and in the final months before the conflict began, the government had a wide knowledge of the United Irishmen's plans

R

through a series of arrests and the work of informers. The rebellion broke out in Wexford in late May of 1798 and there was also fighting in counties Offaly, Carlow, Kildare, Wicklow and Meath, where in many cases the killings were of a sectarian nature. In August of that year a small force of one thousand French troops led by General Jean Humbert won a couple of battles in Mayo before being defeated at Ballinamuck in County Longford. In any case they had arrived after the main thrust of the rebellion was over. Fighting in the north began with an assault on Larne on 6 June, and there were victories over government forces at Ballymena and Randalstown. However, the United Irishmen were decisively beaten at the Battle of Antrim, with many killed and a number of survivors executed. At Saintfield, County Down, government forces were defeated by the insurgents, but at Ballynahinch it was a different story as overwhelming numbers and superior firepower crushed the rebel forces encamped in the town. Estimates vary as to how many died during the rebellion, but one assessment puts the toll at more than twenty thousand. A wave of imprisonments and state executions followed, and ironically, the chief result of the insurrection was the passing of the Act of Union in 1800 which tied Britain and Ireland more closely than ever before.

See also Act of Union, Harp, Republicanism, United Irishmen

Rector

A rector is an ordained Church of Ireland priest in charge of a parish. Historically, the post of rector was slightly different to that of vicar (the more common Church of England term for the priest of the parish) but today the two terms are generally thought to be synonymous. There is a tradition in some Church of Ireland parishes that the priest in charge is known as the vicar, but in most cases the term used is rector.

See also Church of Ireland, Curate, Parish, Priest

R

Red Branch Knights

A gathering of skilled warriors, which included the legendary Cú Chulainn, who were the defenders of Ulster during the reign of King Conchobar Mac Nessa. They were based at Emain Macha (Navan Fort), and a village near the site still bears the name of Creeveroe, an anglicisation of *craobh ruadh*, which is Irish for 'red branch'. The Ulster Cycle of Tales, which tells of the exploits of the Red Branch knights, is sometimes also known as the Red Branch Cycle of Tales.

See also Cattle Raid of Cooley, Cú Chulainn, Deirdre of the Sorrows, Navan Fort, Ulster Cycle of Tales

Red Hand

Representing the nine counties of the province of Ulster in nationalist symbolism, and the six counties of Northern Ireland within unionist symbolism, the red hand has its origins in the official seals of the O'Neills, kings of Ulster in the fourteenth century. It is uncertain why the O'Neills adopted the red hand as their symbol, although two apocryphal stories do offer some suggestions. One is that Hugh O'Neill was inspired to adopt the symbol after seeing a hand on the Monasterboice high cross and being told that it represented the hand of God supporting the Christian church. The other – probably the better known of the two stories – concerns an attempt by one of the O'Neills to capture a piece of land. He was racing a rival across a stretch of water in a bid to be the first to reach the land and in a moment of desperation he cut off his left hand and threw it onto the shore. Since his hand touched the shore first, O'Neill claimed the territory as his own. Although the red hand is more closely associated today with the loyalist tradition (it was adopted as the symbol of the Ulster Volunteer Force in its resistance to home rule in 1913), it has also been employed by the Irish Transport and General Workers' Union, the Irish Citizen Army and the Ancient Order of Hibernians.

See also Ancient Order of Hibernians, Nationalism, Unionism

R

Reel

A four–four dance form imported from Scotland, where many of the first reels were composed in the mid-eighteenth century. A considerable number of the best-known Irish reels are Scottish in origin, and most will have more than one name. Any reel may have up to six different titles, and one, 'The Perthshire Hunt', has at least sixty other names. It has been estimated that there are three times as many titles for reels as there are tunes. The reel is probably the most popular form of instrumental for traditional music in Ireland because its speed and intricacies allow the performer to display his or her musicianship to the full.

See also Jig

Remembrance Sunday

An act of solemn tribute to those who were killed in both world wars and other conflicts which is held at war memorials in towns and villages across the United Kingdom each November. From 1919 until 1945 the act of remembrance was held on Armistice Day, 11 November, which was the anniversary of the signing of the armistice between Britain and Germany at the end of World War I. Armistice Day was renamed Remembrance Sunday after the end of World War II and since 1956 has been held annually on the second Sunday in November. The event is characterised by a two minutes' silence at 11 a.m., a wreath-laying ceremony, and the recitation of lines

R

from 'For the Fallen', a poem written by British poet Laurence Binyon in 1914:

> They shall grow not old, as we that are left grow old:
> Age shall not weary them, nor the years condemn.
> At the going down of the sun and in the morning
> We will remember them.

See also Royal British Legion

Republicanism

The birth of militant Irish republicanism is generally believed to have taken place in May 1795 at McArt's Fort on Cave Hill near Belfast, when Theobald Wolfe Tone and a group of United Irishmen made a pledge 'never to desist in our efforts until we had subverted the authority of England over our country and asserted her independence'. Republicanism, in which the supreme power of the state rests with the elected representatives of the people, rather than with a monarch, was founded in France following the revolution in 1789, and was one of the inspirations of the United Irishmen and their failed rebellion nine years later. An Irish Republic was proclaimed by Patrick Pearse on Easter Monday, 1916, and it was the military actions of Irish republicans which earned the first measure of independence for Ireland in 1921. The twenty-six counties of the Irish Free State officially became a republic in 1949 but republicans remain committed to ensuring that all thirty-two counties of Ireland are united within a single state. The republican movement has been prone to divisive splits caused by differing visions of an all-Ireland republic and the means by which it can be achieved. The modern debate over whether an Irish republic should be pursued by

R

political or military means (or a combination of both) has been a central part of the republican agenda since the IRA split into Official and Provisional wings in 1970. Since it is an ideology born of revolution, republicanism is generally regarded as a more extreme form of Irish nationalism, although there are distinct differences between the two. Republicanism has a very definite political goal, whereas broad national unification is the primary aim of nationalism. At its purest, republicanism adopts an international, non-sectarian view, while nationalism tends to foster a sense of national identity and culture. Republicanism, with its strong socialist subtext, is also more widely associated with the working class, and the concepts of martyrdom and sacrifice are a significant feature of its history and commemoration.

See also Easter Rising, Fenians, Free State, Hunger Strikes, Internment, Loyalism, Nationalism, Rebellion of 1798, Unionism, United Irishmen

Retreat

A tradition observed largely within the Catholic church in which members will withdraw from everyday life and take time to reflect and pray. A retreat usually involves going to a place other than the home, and may be undertaken on an individual basis or as part of a parish or school group. Some retreats may be characterised by the necessity for silence during the period of meditation. Catholic priests are obliged to undertake one week's retreat every year.

See also Priest

Road Bowls

Also known as bullets, this skilful game was played all over Ireland up until the nineteenth century, but now survives chiefly in only two counties – Armagh and Cork. A game is known as a 'score' and involves two participants throwing a twenty-eight-ounce iron ball over a road course of

R

around three miles. The player who completes the course in the least number of throws is the winner. The game was usually played on an informal and locally agreed basis until 1963 when *Bol-Chumann na hÉireann*, the sport's governing body, was formed and official rules were drawn up. All-Ireland championships are now played alternately in Armagh and Cork, and there are also international competitions involving players of similar games throughout Europe. The origin of bullets is uncertain. One theory is that Dutch soldiers brought the game to Ireland and played it with cannon balls during the Williamite Wars (it is still popular in the Netherlands today). Another theory is based on the fact that a game similar to bullets was played by weavers in the mill towns in the north of England, and it was brought to Ireland by immigrant weavers who travelled to the linen-producing areas of Cork and Armagh.

Rosary

A series of prayers accompanied by meditations on the life of Jesus, Mary and Joseph, which is commonly used within the Catholic church. The rosary is divided into 'decades' which consist of a recital of the Our Father (Lord's Prayer), ten Hail Marys and a concluding 'Glory be to the Father, the Son and the Holy Spirit …' An entire rosary is the recital of fifteen decades, and rosary beads are used to count off the decades as they are said. It is believed the tradition of saying the rosary dates back to monastic times when monks would have recited all 150 psalms within the course of a week. At that time many people could not read and were unable to recite anything so complex, so the rosary with its simple prayers was devised as a kind of 'poor man's Psalter' to allow common folk to become part of the tradition.

See also Hail Mary

R

Round Tower

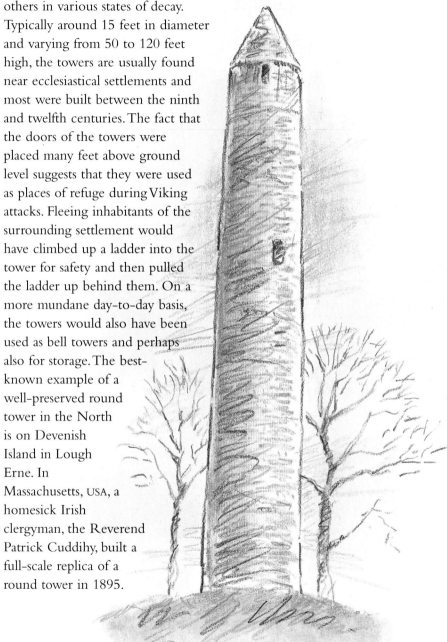

Approximately seventy round towers are said to exist in Ireland, some of them well preserved and others in various states of decay. Typically around 15 feet in diameter and varying from 50 to 120 feet high, the towers are usually found near ecclesiastical settlements and most were built between the ninth and twelfth centuries. The fact that the doors of the towers were placed many feet above ground level suggests that they were used as places of refuge during Viking attacks. Fleeing inhabitants of the surrounding settlement would have climbed up a ladder into the tower for safety and then pulled the ladder up behind them. On a more mundane day-to-day basis, the towers would also have been used as bell towers and perhaps also for storage. The best-known example of a well-preserved round tower in the North is on Devenish Island in Lough Erne. In Massachusetts, USA, a homesick Irish clergyman, the Reverend Patrick Cuddihy, built a full-scale replica of a round tower in 1895.

R

Royal Arch Purple

A senior loyal order coexisting with the Orange institution, the Royal Arch Purple derives its name from 'arch', meaning 'chief' (as in archangel) and its colour from scriptural origins (the curtains of the tabernacle which surrounded the Ark of the Covenant were coloured purple). In everywhere but Ireland the Arch Purple is an integral part of the Orange Order, but in Ireland the Grand Royal Arch Purple Chapter was formed as a separate institution in 1911, and its members have met annually ever since. To be a member of the Royal Arch Purple, you must first be a member of an Orange lodge. District lecturers from the Arch Purple instruct candidates and initiate them as members following a scripture-based ritual. Most members of the Orange Order are also members of the Royal Arch Purple, since it is a natural progression through the institution.

See also Orange Order, Tabernacle

Royal Black Institution

The Imperial Grand Black Chapter cites the date of its formation as 16 September 1797, but it did not become a fully constituted organisation until 1820. The institution was thrown into disarray during the period 1836–46 when, following the dissolution of the Grand Orange Lodge of Ireland, the Grand Black Lodge in Dublin was also dissolved, and the movement split into three, with each branch claiming to be the parent body. In 1846 a meeting in Portadown, County Armagh, reunited most strands of the organisation. Initially, the creation of the Black Institution was greeted with hostility by the Orange Order, mainly because the Orange organisation was led by the nobility while the Black preceptories tended to recruit from the working classes. More scripture-based and less politically involved than the Orange Order, the Black Institution nevertheless has the same hierarchical structures as the Orange Order and uses Orange halls for its meetings. Around one-third of all Orangemen are also members of the Black Institution, and to be accepted for

R

membership a candidate must first be a member of the Orange Order and the Royal Arch Purple. Once accepted, a new member becomes Sir Knight, the equivalent of Brother in the Orange Order, and must complete an elaborate sequence of degrees. Each degree is based on a piece of scripture and has a colour, mystical numbers and certain emblems associated with it. When a member has completed all eleven degrees he becomes a Knight of the Red Cross and is eligible to hold office within the preceptory. Blackmen traditionally held their annual procession on 12 August, commemorating the relief of Derry and the Battle of Newtownbutler, but this date was subsequently altered to the last Saturday in August, a trade holiday in Belfast, which meant that more workers were able to attend the event. Only preceptories in Fermanagh continue to march on the Saturday nearest to 12 August, because of the defeat of a Jacobite force by Enniskillen defenders at Newtownbutler.

See also Knights of Malta, Orange Order, Royal Arch Purple, Sash

Royal British Legion

A welfare organisation for ex-servicemen and women who were personnel in the British or Commonwealth forces. The British Legion's main role revolves around providing assistance with housing and employment problems and it also runs homes for the sick and the elderly. The legion was founded in 1921 by Earl Haig, commander in chief of the British Expeditionary Force during World War I. Poppies made by legion members are sold in the days leading up to Remembrance Sunday to raise revenue for the Earl Haig Fund.

See also Remembrance Sunday

R

Royal Scottish Pipe Band Association

The considerable popularity of highland piping and drumming in Northern Ireland is a visible demonstration of the continuing cultural and historical affinity that has existed for centuries between north-eastern Ireland and Scotland. There are currently around two thousand registered pipers in Northern Ireland – more per head of population than in any other country in the world, including Scotland – and each year there are ten local outdoor competitions for pipe bands plus a number of smaller competitive events. In the early days Northern Ireland pipe bands had their own small representative organisation within the North of Ireland Bands Association, which was superseded by the formation of a Northern Ireland branch of the Scottish Pipe Band Association in 1950. The Scottish association had been created in 1930 and the prefix 'Royal' was granted in 1980. At the time of the formation of the Northern Ireland branch there were just ten local bands, but now there are some one hundred affiliated pipe bands, making Northern Ireland one of the association's largest branches. In the Republic of Ireland, the Irish Pipe Band Association is also affiliated to the Royal Scottish Pipe Band Association.

See also Bagpipes

Rugby

The most commonly held belief about rugby is that the game was invented in Rugby school

R

117

in England in 1823 when a young pupil called William Webb Ellis suddenly picked up the ball during a game of football and ran with it instead of kicking it. There is a theory, however, that Webb was inspired to take this action by his experiences of a Celtic game called cad, which he may have learned from his cousins in County Tipperary. According to the highly speculative hypothesis, cad was a game played at one time throughout the British Isles, and although it was largely supplanted by soccer in England, it continued to be popular in Ireland until the late nineteenth century. The name cad is taken from a Celtic word meaning 'scrotum of the bull', and the ball that was used in the game was very similar in shape to a rugby ball. Proponents of this theory (chief among them was a Kerry parish priest, the Reverend Liam Ferris) believe that rugby is the direct descendant of cad, and therefore a true Gaelic game, while Gaelic football is a modification of soccer. The first Irish rugby club, and the second oldest in the world, was founded at Trinity College Dublin in 1854, but it was six years before another club was formed and the first inter-club match took place. The game began to spread quickly in Dublin and Belfast around this time. In Ulster a rugby section of North of Ireland Cricket Club in Belfast was formed in 1859, although not without initial opposition from the cricketers. The Irish Football Union (the word 'rugby' was added later) was formed in 1874, and the Northern Football Union of Ireland, a body set up to support and promote the game in the north of the country, was founded a year later. There was some rivalry between the two organisations, and for the first international against England in February 1875, the team was made up of an equal number of players drawn from the two unions. However, both bodies amalgamated in 1880 to form the Irish Rugby Football Union (IRFU), which has remained the sport's governing body in Ireland ever since. The first inter-provincial match was played in 1875 between

R

Ulster and Leinster, the two provinces which have dominated Irish rugby since its inception. Although there is a popular perception of rugby as a Protestant and English game, some notable players have included the nationalist stalwart Kevin Barry, who played for University College Dublin Rugby Club, Michael Cusack, one of the co-founders of the GAA, who was both an accomplished rugby player and coach, and Eamon de Valera, the noted republican leader, later *taoiseach* and finally president of Ireland. During the 1916 Easter Rising, in one of history's ironies, IRFU president Frederick Browning was killed by men under the command of Eamon de Valera.

See also Cricket, Gaelic Football, Soccer

Ruling Elder

A lay member of the kirk session, or local governing body, of a Presbyterian church. Elders are elected by members of their congregation and ordained for life by the local presbytery. They are involved in a variety of spiritual and temporal matters within the life of their church and may also be elected to serve on the synod or General Assembly. Despite their title, elders need not necessarily be older members of the congregation.

See also General Assembly, Kirk Session, Presbyterian Church, Presbytery, Synod

R

Sacred Heart of Jesus

A Catholic focus of devotion which goes back to the Middle Ages. It became popular after visions of the wounded heart of the crucified Jesus were witnessed by Saint Margaret Mary Alacoque in seventeenth-century France. The wounded heart came to symbolise not only Christ's humanity but also his great love for his people. The Sacred Heart and the wounds of Jesus became a popular subject for religious artists and later began to be reproduced as an object of devotion for the home. Occasionally, the Sacred Heart icon may be lit by a red lamp. The Feast of the Sacred Heart is observed on the Friday of the week after Corpus Christi.

See also Corpus Christi, Novena, Pioneer Total Abstinence Association

Saint Brigid's Cross

Saint Brigid's crosses can take many different forms, but the one most commonly seen consists of four spokes of equal length radiating from the corners of a central square. Usually made of rushes or straw, the crosses can often be found near household doorways, windows and roofs, where they are placed to bring a blessing on the house. The origins of the cross are unclear but it is said that Saint Brigid, known for her powers of healing, was plaiting a cross from rushes as she tended a dying pagan chieftain. When the chieftain asked what she was doing, Brigid explained the symbolic power of the cross, and the chieftain was so enraptured that he converted to Christianity before he died. Saint Brigid's crosses are traditionally made on the saint's feast day, 1 February, and are sometimes known as Candlemas crosses because they were usually blessed on the day after they were made, Candlemas Day.

S

Saint Patrick

Practically all that is known with any degree of certainty about the patron saint of Ireland is gleaned from the Book of Armagh, whose pages contain the Confession of Patrick and two biographies, although some details have also been found in a few other documents. Patrick's association with Ireland began when he was snatched from his home on the west coast of Britain by an Irish raiding party and brought to a place said to be the slopes of Slemish, County Antrim. During the six years Patrick spent there tending sheep he developed a profound religious belief, and after fleeing bondage and returning to Britain, a vision persuaded him to go back to Ireland once more. Patrick took holy orders and returned to Ireland in AD 432, when it is said that he founded his first church in a barn at Saul, County Down (Saul is a corruption of the Irish word *sabhall*, meaning 'barn'). A local chieftain, Dichu, became the saint's first convert after he had been rendered powerless during an attempt to strike Patrick with his sword. Although not the first Christian missionary to visit Ireland, Patrick was certainly the most successful; he made many converts, established churches and spread the word of God rapidly without the creation of any martyrs. Saint Patrick is reputed to be buried in Downpatrick, County Down, alongside Saint Brigid and Saint Colmcille, although there is little hard evidence to support this claim. His feast day on 17 March, an occasion for parades and pilgrimages at locations throughout Ireland and around the world, is said to have been fixed by a Franciscan scholar, Father Luke Wadding, although a more entertaining story has it that a priest resolved the bitter dispute over whether Saint Patrick's Day should be on 8 or 9 March by simply adding the two dates together.

S

See also Ancient Order of Hibernians, Book of Armagh, Shamrock

Saint Vincent de Paul

A Catholic lay organisation founded in 1833 to help the poor and disadvantaged within local parishes. The organisation was inspired by the charitable works of the seventeenth-century French saint, Vincent de Paul, who devoted his life to the care of the sick and the poor and set up the Congregation of Mission Priests in 1625 and the Daughters of Charity in 1633. Today members of the society will often hold collections outside churches after a service and use the money raised to help local needy people.

Samhain

A Celtic precursor to the festival of Hallowe'en, which would have consisted of feasting and entertainment but would also have been a lament for the passing of summer, and perhaps also for friends and family members who had recently died. *Samhain* is the Irish language word for the month of November.

See also Bealtaine, Celts, Hallowe'en, Lughnasa

Sash

Although it is making a comeback in Orange and Black circles, the sash is seen at demonstrations today much less often than in days gone by. The more favoured symbol of Orange Order or Black Preceptory membership is the collarette. The collarette was originally designed for use inside the Orange hall while the sash would be worn at outside parades. Both of these items replaced scarves or ribbons which were worn in the early days of the loyal orders.

S

Gradually, the more convenient and neater-fitting collarette replaced the sash as the favoured badge of membership at processions. Orange Order collarettes and sashes are usually adorned with a badge denoting the member's lodge number, plus (often incorrectly) other symbols from the Royal Arch Purple and the Black Institution. Formerly, men who were members of both the Orange Order and Black Institution wore the two sashes, one over each shoulder, when marching on the Twelfth. The former Orange leader, William Johnston of Ballykilbeg, was depicted wearing three sashes in 1867 – Orange and Black sashes plus the crimson sash of the Apprentice Boys of Derry.

See also Apprentice Boys of Derry, Orange Order, Royal Arch Purple, Royal Black Institution, Twelfth of July

Scór

The *Scór* (an Irish language word meaning 'score') is a wide-ranging cultural competition founded in County Down in the late 1960s and now administered by the GAA throughout Ireland. Divided into two age categories, *Scór na nÓg*, for the under seventeens, and *Scór na Sinsear*, for adults above that age, the competition encompasses a variety of disciplines, including *céilí* and set dancing, recitation, solo singing and instrumental music, as well as a quiz, novelty acts and a performance by a ballad group. Strict rules for the instrumental music section state that a piece of music must be performed by between three and five persons, and no electrical instruments are permitted – although it is rumoured that enterprising keyboard players have been able to circumvent the regulations by using battery-powered instruments. Competitors are chosen to represent their local GAA club at county level, and, if successful, they then progress to provincial finals, and finally to all-Ireland finals. The all-Ireland *Scór* finals in 1993 were held in the same venue as the Eurovision Song Contest that same year, Millstreet in County Cork. The *Scór* finals attracted an audience of six hundred more people.

See also Gaelic Athletic Association

S

Scout Movement

There are two main scouting traditions in Northern Ireland: the Scout Association, regulated by the Northern Ireland Scout Council, and the thirty-two-county Scouting Ireland CSI, formerly known as the Catholic Boy Scouts of Ireland (CBSI). Both organisations have their origins in the Boy Scout Association which was founded in England by Robert Baden-Powell in 1908. In that same year the first scout troops were formed in the north of Ireland under the auspices of Baden-Powell's fledgling organisation, and it is these groups which formed the nucleus of the body regulated by the Northern Ireland Scout Council today. The CBSI, meanwhile, was inspired by the work of Greystones Catholic curate, Father Ernest Farrell, who in the mid-1920s founded a boys' parochial group whose members wore scout-like uniforms. The organisation was officially inaugurated as the Catholic Boy Scouts of Ireland by Ernest's brother, Father Tom Farrell, in Dublin in 1927. Both organisations have oaths of allegiance, or 'promises' as they are more commonly known. The Scout Association promise requires allegiance to 'God and the Queen' while the Scouting Ireland promise declares allegiance to the principles of Catholicism, although this has been modified recently to accommodate non-Catholic members. Scouting Ireland is organised under the auspices of the local Catholic church and is administered in regions which roughly correspond to church dioceses, while the Scout Association organises its groups according to the county boundaries. Although they are strictly non-denominational, Scout Association groups may sometimes be sponsored by a local church (quite often the Church of Ireland) although a large proportion of groups have no connection with any one church. Both organisations are now open to boys and girls, having dropped the word 'boy' from their titles, although each tradition continues to maintain separate guide movements for girls only.

See also Boys' Brigade

Sean-nós

A comparatively recent musical term, coined within the past thirty or forty years to describe a highly embellished form of unaccompanied singing. *Sean-nós* literally means 'old style' and this type of singing is common in all the *Gaeltacht* areas, each having its own style of singing. The songs sung in this fashion can be in both the English and Irish languages.

See also Gaeltacht

Select Vestry

Every year around Easter, Church of Ireland parishes hold a general vestry meeting (effectively the AGM of the parish) at which parishioners elect a group of people to the select vestry to carry on the general business of the parish. Church wardens, senior lay people with specific roles within the parish, are also elected at the vestry meeting.

See also Church of Ireland, Parish

Session

An informal gathering of musicians playing a variety of instruments. At these occasions there is no predetermined list of tunes to be played. One or two musicians will simply start a well-known tune and the rest will join in. At some point during the music a different tune will be introduced without stopping, and again the rest of the players will follow. Three or four tunes are usually played in one continuous flow before there is a break. Sessions are mainly for instrumental music only and singers generally take a back seat unless they are called

S

upon for a song. The holding of traditional music sessions in pubs is a very recent phenomenon. Up until the early 1960s sessions usually took place in people's houses or at a local hall, while most pubs actively discouraged them.

Set Dancing

Set dancing originated in the quadrilles brought from France to England and Ireland by soldiers who served in the Napoleonic Wars. Quadrilles are so called because couples dance in a square formation facing each other, and they were a popular and fashionable pastime in Paris in the nineteenth century. The music to accompany the quadrilles was usually played in the same tempo as much Irish dance music, so when the new dances were brought to Ireland it proved a simple matter to substitute jigs and reels, and in time local dance steps were also added. The dances were initially known as sets of quadrilles, later shortened to 'sets' when four couples took part, and 'half-sets' when there were only two couples. Various local versions with their own distinctive names developed and set dancing became one of the most popular entertainments in Ireland until well into the twentieth century. After a lull in interest, set dancing is once again enjoying a boom in popularity.

See also Jig, Reel

Sham Fight

A re-enactment of the Battle of the Boyne held annually at Scarva in County Down on 13 July. Scarva was the location of the headquarters of William III's army as it mustered for the advance towards the Boyne in 1690 after having been dispersed in winter quarters throughout Ulster. The Battle of the Boyne has been refought (with always the same outcome) at Scarva every year since at least 1835. In the early years of the re-enactment, Newry canal stood in for the Boyne and occasionally

participants would get so carried away by events that serious injuries, and even deaths, resulted.

See also Battle of the Boyne

Shamrock

The most instantly recognisable symbol of Ireland, shamrock is a collective name for a number of different varieties of three-leaved plants. The word comes from the Irish *seamróg*, meaning 'clover', and is usually taken to refer to the lesser yellow trefoil, *Trifolium minus*. The earliest depictions of the shamrock in Ireland can be found in Celtic art. They were illustrated in the Book of Kells and can be found engraved on some stone crosses. Legend has it that Saint Patrick used the shamrock to demonstrate the three-in-one doctrine of the Trinity during his conversion of the Irish to Christianity, a tradition perpetuated since the seventeenth century with the wearing of shamrock on Saint Patrick's Day. Although often regarded as a symbol of nationalism, the shamrock has been employed as an emblem by a broad sweep of political

S

opinion. The mostly Protestant militia of the 1780s, the Volunteers, used it widely on flags and medals, and it was a common insignia used by both sides during the 1798 rebellion. Medals minted to commemorate the Act of Union in 1801 intertwined the shamrock with the symbolically English oak leaf, while the Fenians often depicted thirty-two shamrock leaves in their imagery to signify the number of Irish counties. In the United States, a naval vessel named the USS *Shamrock* was christened with a bottle of Irish whiskey on Saint Patrick's Day 1863 and presented with a wreath of shamrock.

See also Act of Union, Fenians, Rebellion of 1798, Saint Patrick

Shinty

A game similar to hurling which is played mostly in the Highlands and on the west coast of Scotland. The ancient connection between the Glens of Antrim and the west of Scotland led to elements of the game crossing the North Channel, and in some places in north Antrim hurling was generally known as shinty or 'shinny'. In the National Museum in Dublin there are examples of north Antrim shinty sticks on display. Played on a pitch about the same size as a hurling pitch, shinty involves two teams of twelve players using sticks which are more like hockey sticks than hurleys. As a result, there is more play with the ball on the ground in shinty than there is with hurling. The goals are known as 'hails'. It is said that the earliest shinty matches in Scotland were usually rough encounters between clans or parishes, with the players fired up by rousing bagpipe music and liberal quantities of whisky. However, the drawing up of official rules in 1887, and the setting up of a governing body in 1893, helped to smooth out the rough edges, and in 1897 the first match between Scottish shinty players and Irish hurlers took place in Glasgow. Challenge matches continue to be played annually.

See also Cricket, Hockey, Hurling

S

Shrine

A place of prayer with some particular visual focus, such as a statue, picture or relic, found either inside a Catholic church or at an outdoor location. Among the best known shrines within the Catholic tradition are those at Lourdes, Fatima and Knock, and the design of many smaller local shrines may be inspired by these larger ones. Pilgrimages to particularly revered shrines are regularly organised by Catholic parishes. Candles will often be lit by those who come to pray and then placed beside the shrine.

Siege of Derry

The focus of the campaign by the Catholic James II to regain the English throne from the Protestant king, William of Orange, was centred on Ireland when James landed at Kinsale in Cork County with an army of French soldiers in 1689, intending to use Ireland as a springboard for a return to power in England. In the closing weeks of 1688 the Jacobite force of Lord Antrim's Redshanks had attempted to capture the city of Derry, but thirteen apprentice boys ignored advice from leading citizens who feared that resistance was

S

129

futile, and they shut the gates to the walled city on 18 December. The siege proper did not begin until April 1689 when James arrived at Derry and was refused entry. Over the next 105 days the city's thirty thousand inhabitants were reduced by two-thirds through starvation, bombardment and disease. Cats, dogs, mice and rats were all eaten by the besieged Protestants before the city was finally relieved on 12 August by a small fleet of British ships which sailed up Lough Foyle.

See also Apprentice Boys of Derry, Battle of the Boyne, Lundy

Skittles

A rural crossroads game that appears to have its origins in the Middle Ages and is still played today, largely in east Down, Fermanagh and Cavan. Two teams compete with each other to knock five vertical pieces of wood, called 'standers', out of a five-foot-wide target ring using four wooden throwing skittles. The throwing line which the player must stand behind is known as the 'spud' and the wood from which the throwing sticks are made is traditionally either ash or oak. Sometimes the skittles are soaked in water before they are thrown to give them better weight and to stop them from splitting. The game was often played at fairs and festivals and was popular throughout much of Ireland up until the beginning of the twentieth century. As with so many traditional country games, the rules varied from locality to locality, but in recent times a set of standard rules has been drawn up and all-Ireland championships were inaugurated in 1976.

Slim

An often-used name for potato bread, which is made from a dough of cooked potatoes and flour and traditionally baked on a cast-iron griddle over an open fire. The term 'slim' probably comes from the method of preparation, which involves rolling the potato dough thinly before cutting it into portions for baking. In some parts of Ireland there is a variety of slim called boxty, from the Irish word *bocht* meaning 'poor', since potato bread was often regarded as a poor man's dish.

See also Potato, Ulster Fry

Soccer

Soccer, a colloquial term for association football, shares its ancient origins with Gaelic football and rugby in a game played in Britain and Ireland as early as the seventh or eighth century AD. From these times up until the nineteenth century, football would have been played in a wide variety of local forms, the most common being a loosely organised inter-parish match played across fields and open country. The size of teams would have varied, as would the rules, which would have been laid down according to local tradition and agreed between the teams before the start of the game. The earliest recorded evidence of any kind of football match in Ireland refers to a contest in Slane, County Meath, in the middle of the seventeenth century. Two hundred years later, football effectively split into three branches in Ireland, with the formation of the various governing bodies for soccer, Gaelic football and rugby, and the drawing up of official rules for each game. Unlike rugby and Gaelic football, soccer is divided into two separately governed leagues in Ireland: the Irish League features professional and semi-professional teams from the North while the League of Ireland is made up of teams in the Republic, and occasionally some teams from the North, such as

S

Derry City. The Irish League, founded in the Belfast estate office of the Marquis of Dufferin and Ava on 14 March 1880, initially had jurisdiction over the whole of Ireland, but with the creation of the border in 1921 the southern clubs withdrew and formed the Irish Free State Football Association and the League of Ireland. During the years when there was one league for the whole island, Irish soccer was dominated by the northern clubs and up until the split no club outside Belfast had won the Irish League championship. International soccer in Ireland also has two ruling bodies: the Irish Football Association in the North and the Football Association of Ireland (the successor to the Irish Free State Football Association) in the South. Both field a team in world competitions, but as recently as the 1970s the Northern Ireland team was often described simply as 'Ireland' in official programmes for home internationals (involving games against England, Scotland and Wales) and only became 'Northern Ireland' for games against countries outside the United Kingdom. Nowadays, references to 'Ireland' invariably relate to the Republic of Ireland team.

See also Gaelic Football,
Partition, Rugby

Society of Friends *see* Quakers

Soda Bread

An unleavened bread made from a mixture of flour and buttermilk which in days gone by was baked over an open fire using a cast-iron griddle. It is called soda bread because bicarbonate of soda is used instead of yeast to make the bread rise. The continued popularity of home-made soda bread has ensured the easy availability of buttermilk (the left-over liquid in butter production) in Northern Ireland shops while it has disappeared from the shelves almost everywhere else.

See also Ulster Fry

S

The Soldier's Song

First published in 1912, the words to 'The Soldier's Song' were written by Peadar Kearney, the author of a number of political songs and a member of the Irish Republican Brotherhood (forerunner of the IRA). Despite a variety of efforts to find a suitable anthem for the newly formed Irish Free State, it was not until 1926 that 'The Soldier's Song' was officially adopted. The version most frequently played today is actually only the chorus of the song, and the verses have been largely forgotten. (At the World Cup soccer finals in the USA in 1994, much confusion was caused when American bands played the melody of the verses before the chorus at matches involving the Irish team.) Although an English translation of the words of the song does exist, it is nowadays mostly sung in Irish, to a translation by Liam Ó Rinn published in 1923. Ó Rinn's version caused controversy shortly after its publication because his translation of the first line 'Soldiers are we' to '*Sinne Fianna Fáil*' seemed to imply a connection between the state's anthem and Eamon de Valera's Fianna Fáil party. This, however, could not have been the case since the words were published three years before Fianna Fáil was founded.

See also Fenians, National Anthem

Solemn League and Covenant

A document created by Sir Edward Carson in response to the movement towards home rule for Ireland in 1912. Signatories of the Solemn League and Covenant pledged to defend 'our cherished position of equal citizenship within the United Kingdom' and to resist all attempts at home rule. Ulster Day was designated as 28 September 1912, when demonstrations across the North accompanied mass signings of the Solemn League and Covenant. Only men were allowed to sign the covenant (another document was drawn up for women) but of the 471,414 signatures collected on Ulster Day, more came from women than from men.

See also Easter Rising, Home Rule, Partition, Stormont

S

Starry Plough

Devised by the nationalist poet George Russell, and created by artist William H. Megahey, the Starry Plough was originally intended to be used as the flag of the Irish labour movement, but it was adopted by the Irish Citizen Army, which had been formed by members of the Irish Transport and General Workers' Union, and was first flown in 1914. When the Easter Rising took place two years later, the Starry Plough was flown during the fighting from the roof of the Imperial Hotel in Dublin.

See also Easter Rising, Red Hand

Stations of the Cross

A series of fourteen devotional works of art positioned on the interior walls of a Catholic church depicting various scenes from Jesus' condemnation by Pontius Pilate to him being placed in the tomb. The devotion of the Stations of the Cross was brought back to Europe by pilgrims who followed Christ's journey to the cross through Jerusalem and rested at various points, known as 'stations', where a particular incident is believed to have happened. The depictions of these incidents in Catholic churches allow worshippers to spiritually participate in that pilgrimage. A more recent historical development has seen the addition of a fifteenth station representing the resurrection.

Stormont

When George V opened the first parliament of Northern Ireland on 22 June 1921, it was not at

S

Stormont buildings, but at Belfast City Hall, where the parliament initially met. It was not until 1932 that the neo-classical parliament buildings at Stormont were officially inaugurated by the Prince of Wales. The Northern Ireland parliament at Stormont was the first devolved government of its kind in the United Kingdom. It was modelled fairly closely upon Westminster, with a fifty-two-member House of Commons, and an upper house, the Senate, with twenty-four members together with the lord mayor of Belfast and the mayor of Derry. Stormont assumed responsibility for a range of government tasks previously administered from London, ironically giving unionists a version of home rule that they had vigorously resisted only ten years previously. Initially, the Stormont parliament was only in session for short periods on two or three days per week, but gradually the workload increased. The first cabinet in 1921 consisted of just seven MPs, but had more than doubled to fifteen by 1971. Regarded by nationalists as a symbol of unionist dominance, and by unionists as an emblem of the permanence of the northern state, Stormont buildings served as the seat of Northern Ireland government until 1972 when direct rule was imposed by Westminster. Since that time it has been the setting for a number of failed devolved assemblies.

See also Gerrymander, Home Rule, Partition, Unionism

S

Sunday School

Sunday schools were set up by a variety of Protestant churches from the late eighteenth century onwards to provide religious instruction for children of the local congregation. In their early days Sunday schools would also have provided a basic education in secular subjects. In the early nineteenth century a number of Sunday school unions were formed in Ireland to provide support for schools of different denominations, but many of these were eventually broken up by inter-faith differences. Today most Sunday schools are run under the auspices of the local parish or congregation.

Synod

The General Synod of the Church of Ireland is the supreme administrative body of the church, and is composed of clergy and lay people under the presidency of the archbishop of Armagh. The Church of Ireland Diocesan Synod is the governing body of the diocese and is also composed of clergy and laity under the presidency of the bishop. In Presbyterianism, the term synod corresponds roughly with the episcopal term diocese, in that a number of presbyteries make up a synod and a number of synods make up the General Assembly. The synod is made up of ministers and representative elders from two or more presbyteries within its area. In the early days of Presbyterianism in Ireland, the whole of Ulster was one synod. A Methodist district synod is attended by representatives from church circuits and meets twice a year under the chairmanship of a minister elected for a three-year term. There are eight Methodist synods in Ireland.

See also Cathedral, Church of Ireland, Circuit, General Assembly, Methodist Church, Presbyterian Church, Presbytery

S

Tabernacle

Derived from the Latin word *tabernaculum*, meaning 'tent', the word tabernacle has a variety of meanings within different faiths. In the Catholic church the tabernacle is an ornamental receptacle for the vessels which contain the consecrated bread and wine used in the Eucharist. Often the tabernacle is covered with a veil and a lamp is kept burning in front of it, except during the Easter vigil from Good Friday to Easter Sunday. Within the Jewish faith, the tabernacle is the tent referred to in the Book of Exodus which contained the Ark of the Covenant and was said to have been constructed under the direction of Moses. The word tabernacle is also used to describe a Baptist house of worship.

See also Baptist Church, Catholic Church, Holy Communion, Royal Arch Purple

Táin Bó Cuailnge *see* Cattle Raid of Cooley

Tara Brooch

A famous gold and jewel-encrusted Celtic brooch which, despite its name, has no known connection with the Hill of Tara, the ancient seat of the high kings of Ireland. The eighth-century brooch, which would have been used by either a man or a woman to fasten a cloak, was actually found at Bettystown, County Meath, in 1850. The name 'Tara brooch' was a romantic label coined by a Dublin goldsmith.

T

Tartan

A woollen cloth woven with differently coloured threads at regular intervals to produce a distinctive cross-striped design most commonly seen in Scottish Highland dress. Tartan cloth is traditionally used for making kilts and plaids (a cloak worn over one shoulder). The association of particular tartans with certain clans is said to date from the seventeenth century, but most authorities maintain that the connection between clans and tartan design is largely mythical. The official designation of an Ulster tartan, of which there are two varieties, stems from the discovery of a set of seventeenth-century tartan clothes on a farm at Dungiven, County Londonderry, in 1956. Because it had been buried for some time, the tartan was discoloured by the peaty soil and the colours were difficult to identify. The first attempt to determine the colours of the cloth resulted with the registering of an official brown and red Ulster tartan with the Scottish Tartan Society in the early 1970s, but experts now believe that the more accurate colours of the Ulster tartan are red, green, yellow and black, and this cloth has also been officially registered with the society.

Tin Whistle

A popular instrument for traditional music and ideal for solo performances, although the tin whistle is often not held in very high regard by some traditional musicians. Some see it as a beginner's instrument, from which the proficient progress on to the flute. However, in the hands of an expert the humble mass-produced tin whistle can hold its own against more respected instruments. Although similar instruments have been in existence in most parts of the world for thousands of years, the origins of the tin whistle are fairly obscure. However, the whistle is mentioned

T

in ancient Irish stories which tell how the Tuatha Dé Danaan used the instrument to play 'fairy music' to put their adversaries to sleep. In modern traditional music there is a wide variety of playing styles, some of them influenced by flute and uilleann pipe techniques.

See also Flute, Tuatha Dé Danaan, Uilleann Pipes

Tír na nÓg

A mythical land of eternal youth which features widely in Celtic mythology. Tír na nÓg (literally 'land of the young') is said to be an underground kingdom established by the Tuatha Dé Danaan where no one grows old, everyone is physically beautiful and pain and decay are unknown.

See also Tuatha Dé Danaan

Titanic

There can be few people in the world today who have not heard of the *Titanic* and how she sank on her maiden voyage after striking an iceberg on the night of 14 April 1912. But the vessel's story has become much more than just another shipping disaster; it has become a symbol of the end of an old world order, a forewarning of the slaughter of World War I, and a reminder of the folly of believing in the infallibility of technological achievement. Perhaps nowhere is the symbolism more potent than in her native Belfast, where the tussle for cultural ownership of the largest ship afloat began before her hull had even touched the water. In 1911 the nationalist *Irish News* was

T

proclaiming the ship to be the 'most convincing of proofs of Irish brains and Irish industry', while the unionist *Ulster Echo* declared that *Titanic* and her sister ship *Olympic* 'stand for the pre-eminence of the Anglo-Saxon race on the ocean'. In the years that followed her sinking, however, *Titanic* became firmly lodged in the Protestant psyche alongside the Battle of the Somme as the embodiment of an emotional stew that has pride and loss and heroism and futility among its ingredients. *Titanic* became identified with Protestantism principally because it was built by a Harland and Wolff workforce which was overwhelmingly Protestant. At the time of its construction, Ireland was embroiled in the home rule crisis, which many Protestants were convinced would result in the ultimate break-up of the union. The destruction of the Protestant-built *Titanic* only two days after the third Home Rule Bill was read in the House of Commons seemed an ill omen for those who supported the union. Meanwhile, many Catholics viewed the sinking of the *Titanic* as retribution for those who had harassed and discriminated against their co-religionists at the Belfast shipyard, despite the fact that many Irish Catholics had gone down with the ship.

See also Battle of the Somme, Home Rule

Townland

In the administrative subdivision of land, townlands form the smallest unit, with a number of townlands forming a parish, and a group of parishes forming a barony. Since many early land divisions were of different sizes and based on local knowledge and oral rather than written definitions, the exact origins of townlands are somewhat hazy. It was not until the surveys and map-making exercises of the seventeenth century that the variety of small local land units which had existed up until then were given the general name of townlands. The fact that many townlands do not include any sort of recognisable town at all may be due to the fact that the Irish prefix *baile* (Bally), which is found in many townland names, was equated with the English word 'town', when in fact it may have referred to simply a

T

settlement or even a piece of land. There is no specific size for a townland; in Northern Ireland they can range from just 4 acres up to over 4,000 acres, and the average size of a townland is 357 acres. This vast difference in size is probably due to the fact that in early history land evaluation was based on the proportion of arable land to uncultivated ground within a given area. Larger townlands, therefore, tended to be made up of a greater proportion of poor farming land.

See also Barony, Parish, Placenames

Travellers

Given the nature of travellers to move from one place to another, it is difficult to be certain about their origins and early history. In Ireland and Scotland there has been a tradition of indigenous itinerant craftsmen since the fifth century. Skilled metal workers were known to have travelled the country at this time, and by the fourteenth century, 'tinker' was a common trade listed in official records. English laws were passed on three occasions between the thirteenth and fifteenth centuries to curtail the 'wandering Irish', as they had become known. It seems certain that travellers were so well-established in Ireland and Scotland by the sixteenth century that it was not possible for the eastern European Romany gypsies to become established in either place. There was also considerable movement of travellers between Ireland and Scotland at this time and in the centuries that followed. One of the most commonly held beliefs about the origins of the current traveller families in Ireland is that they are the descendants of people dispossessed from areas that were badly hit by the Famine of the mid-nineteenth century, although it should be stressed that not all families became itinerant in the same way. At the time of the Famine, a number of traveller families emigrated to America where instead of being integrated into their adopted home, they continued their nomadic lifestyle. In Ireland the travelling community remains a closely knit one (a 1960s report revealed that one-third of all travellers share just nine surnames), although there are intense rivalries between some families. It is not possible for a settled person

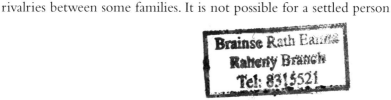

to become a true traveller – one must be born into the life. Weddings and funerals are particularly important occasions, and travellers will often meet at specific annual fairs. The settled community tends to react with suspicion and hostility to the appearance of travellers, although few of the deeply held prejudices of the outside world have much basis in fact.

See also Famine

Tricolour

Tradition has it that the Tricolour was introduced into Ireland in 1848 following a visit to Paris by a deputation of Young Irelanders. There is much evidence to suggest, however, that the flag existed in Ireland for some time before this. In the traditional version of the flag's origin, it is said that the Irish Tricolour was sewn together by the women of Paris as a gesture of solidarity between the two nations, and the flag was intended to symbolise the white of peace between the Orange and the Green in Ireland. Many historians are convinced, however, that the Tricolour had been used by the Young Ireland movement some years before they are supposed to have brought the flag from France. It has even been claimed that the deputation took the flag to France with them and then brought it home again to increase the profile of the Tricolour and to encourage its use. Whatever the truth of the story, the Tricolour did not really come into common use until the end of the nineteenth century, most notably at the centenary commemoration of the 1798 rising. Its most spectacular rise to prominence was when it was flown from the roof of the General Post Office in Dublin during the Easter Rising in 1916. It was also a key symbol of defiance during the War of Independence from 1919 to 1921 before becoming the official flag of the Irish Free State and later, the Republic. In 1972 an Irish Tricolour was placed on the moon by Apollo 17 astronaut, Eugene Cernan.

See also Easter Rising, Free State

Tuatha Dé Danaan

The name given to a mythical people who lived in Ireland before the Celtic settlers arrived. Tradition states that the Tuatha Dé Danaan, the people of the goddess Dana, became supernatural beings and went to live underground in the land of eternal youth, Tír na nÓg, upon the arrival of the Celts. Fairy mounds dotted around the countryside are said to be the domains of their chiefs, and from this arises the rural custom that disturbing a fairy mound will bring bad luck.

See also Celts, Tír na nÓg

Twelfth of July

The annual commemoration of William of Orange's victory at the Battle of the Boyne by members of the Orange Order. Parades are usually held at district or county level, although some districts join together to form a 'combine' for the parade. Venues are usually chosen by rotation and the local lodge or district will be designated as the host. Traditionally, each Orange lodge holds a short march in its own locality on the morning of the Twelfth before travelling to the main parade. In the case of a combine, each district would also have a parade before coming together for the main procession. During the main parade of the day, the lodges of each district march in numerical sequence, interspersed by local bands, to the 'field'. Here, prayers are said and resolutions on loyalty, Orange ideals and current events are proposed. Orange lodges would usually be accompanied by banners painted with depictions of events important to the institution. Banners are a relatively modern introduction, however; until the turn of the century, painted flags were a more common sight at Twelfth demonstrations.

See also Ancient Order of Hibernians, Arch, Banner, Battle of the Boyne, Bowler Hat, Orange Order, Sash

T

Uilleann Pipes

The uilleann or union pipes emerged in Ireland around the beginning of the eighteenth century. *Píb uilleann* means 'bagpipes of the elbows' because the bellows is worked with one elbow, and the other controls the bag. It has been suggested that the name union pipes was derived from the Act of Union in 1801, but this is unlikely as the name was in use long before the act was passed. Instead, the word 'union' seems to refer to a technical unity between two parts of the instrument. Uilleann pipes differ markedly in a number of respects from bagpipes. The air supply is provided by a bellows as opposed to being mouth-blown; the chanter has a range of two octaves as compared to the nine notes of the bagpipe chanter; and by the early nineteenth century it had developed a rhythmic and harmonic accompaniment in the form of the regulators. The uilleann pipes are always played in the sitting position whereas the bagpipes can be played standing or walking. The instrument fell into decline towards the end of the nineteenth century but was revived in the early years of the twentieth century by the establishment of the Cork and Dublin Pipers' Clubs, and by the *Feis Cheoil* and *Oireachtas* piping competitions. Since the founding of *Na Píobairí Uilleann* in 1968 the instrument has begun to prosper once again and is now enjoying unprecedented popularity.

See also Accordion, Act of Union, Bagpipes

Ulster

Named after the Ulaidh, an ancient tribe which once held sway in the northern portion of

Ireland, Ulster is one of the four provinces of Ireland. It consists of nine counties, six of which (Antrim, Armagh, Down, Fermanagh, Londonderry and Tyrone) are in Northern Ireland and the remaining three (Cavan, Donegal and Monaghan) are in the Republic of Ireland. Northern Ireland is often erroneously referred to as 'Ulster' or 'the province' even though it constitutes only two-thirds of the actual province of Ulster. County Louth was at one time considered to be part of Ulster, but it was absorbed into the province of Leinster some time before the seventeenth century. It was the Normans who first coined the term Ulster, when they created the earldom of Ulster centred on Antrim and Down in 1205. Previously, the Vikings had called the region Uladstir, a corruption of the Gaelic *tír Ulaidh*, which means 'land of the Ulaidh'.

See also Loyalism, Normans, Province, Vikings

Ulster Cycle of Tales

A body of early Irish heroic literature, whose central story is the *Táin Bó Cuailnge* (Cattle Raid of Cooley), which tells of the defeat of the warriors of Queen Medbh by Cú Chulainn, the 'hound of Ulster'. Thought to be among the oldest heroic literature in Western Europe, the tales appear to date from the iron age and were handed down orally for many centuries before being recorded in writing by monks in counties Down and Monaghan around the sixth to eighth centuries AD. Although one can only speculate on whether or not the tales are based on actual events, the stories have nevertheless provided much inspiration for Celtic revivalist writers and artists. A translation of the stories into Russian has sold more than 150,000 copies.

See also Cattle Raid of Cooley, Celts, Cú Chulainn, Deirdre of the Sorrows, Navan Fort, Red Branch Knights

145

Ulster Fry

A meal of fried food that includes sausages, bacon, egg and fried bread, with other additions according to taste. Often served as the first meal of the day, the Ulster fry is probably an extension of the English tradition of hearty breakfasts, begun in the Middle Ages, although the Northern Ireland version has established its own unique identity through the mandatory inclusion of fried soda bread and potato bread (slim).

See also Slim, Soda Bread

Ulster-Scots

The Ulster-Scots language, also known as Ullans, is a regional variation of Scots, a language still spoken in the Lowlands of Scotland which shares its roots with standard English but was subject to a different development over the centuries. The Scots tongue, dubbed Lallans (or 'lowlands') by Robert Burns in 1796, was brought to the north-eastern part of Ireland during the plantation in the early seventeenth century. Up until this time Scots had been the official language of the Scottish kingdom. However, following the union of the thrones of England and Scotland in 1707 it began to decline in its written form and became largely a spoken language, although Burns used it extensively in his written work some two hundred years later. The Ulster variant of Scots developed most strongly in those areas where Lowland planters settled in concentrated numbers – Antrim, east Down, north Londonderry and east Donegal – and it is in these areas that most speakers of Ulster-Scots can be found today. Ulster-Scots literature also developed within these areas, most notably in local newspapers and through the writing of the weaver poets and kailyard (literally 'cabbage patch') literature, a type of sentimental rural novel. It has been estimated that there are one hundred thousand people in Ulster who speak Ulster-Scots, although some have suggested that the number may be as low as ten to fifteen thousand, many of whom are elderly. Concerns for the future of Ulster-Scots and its marginalised cultural status prompted the formation of the Ulster-Scots Language Society in 1992 to

U

encourage greater awareness and use of the tongue. The society has been actively involved in the debate over whether or not Ulster-Scots is a language or, as some of its detractors claim, a dialect. Those who argue that Ulster-Scots is a dialect say that its forms are too close to standard English for it to be considered as a separate language, while supporters of Ulster-Scots maintain that it should be recognised as a language because it has its own grammar and vocabulary, a considerable body of literature and its own distinct history of development.

See also Irish Language, Plantation

Unction

A process of anointing a person with oil which forms part of the Catholic sacraments of baptism, confirmation, ordination and anointing of the sick. The anointing of the sick used to be known as Extreme Unction because it was usually carried out when it was felt that the person was close to death. The sacrament is now administered to people who are sick but are not in any danger of death. There is provision within the Anglican church for anointing the sick with oil, but it is rarely used.

Union Jack

Although the term Union Jack is widely used to describe the flag of the United Kingdom, its official name is the Union Flag. The name Union Jack was originally used to describe the flag only when it was flown from the 'jackstaff' (bow) of a ship. Created in 1606, following the union of the crowns of England and Scotland, the first Union Flag depicted the crosses of Saint George and Saint Andrew. It was not until the Act of Union between

Britain and Ireland in 1801 that the red diagonal cross of Saint Patrick was added. The use of the Union Jack as a symbol of loyalty to the British crown was minimal in Ireland until the latter part of the nineteenth century, but it became particularly prominent during the unionist campaign against home rule. At an anti-home-rule demonstration in 1912, unionists displayed what they claimed was the largest Union Jack ever made; it stretched almost the entire width of the interior of the Ulster Hall in Belfast.

See also Act of Union, Home Rule

Unionism

The political creed of those who support the retention of Northern Ireland (the whole of Ireland before 1921) within the United Kingdom. The first unionist political organisation was created following the general election of 1886 in response to growing pressure for Irish home rule. In the latter part of the nineteenth century, unionists tended to embrace the notion of a culturally distinct Ireland locked firmly within the United Kingdom. For example, they felt there was no dichotomy in displaying the slogan, *Erin Go Bragh* ('Ireland for ever', a slogan also used by the United Irishmen one hundred years previously) alongside 'God Save the Queen' at the 1892 Ulster Unionist convention in Belfast, or using Irish emblems such as the harp or shamrock and linking them with a crown to symbolise the union between the two islands. When the home rule question resurfaced in the years before World War I, unionists adopted a more militant stance and became less willing to offer unqualified support for crown and government if it meant the end of the link between Britain and Ireland. Partition offered the only way for the union with at least part of the island to be maintained, and thus began fifty years of devolved government dominated by unionist politics in Northern Ireland. In their political outlook, mainstream unionists have traditionally shared a number of key policies with the British Conservative Party, which in 1909 took the official name of the Conservative and Unionist Party. However, the fact that unionism embraces many different shades of opinion, often only united by a common belief in continuing the link with Britain, became increasingly obvious during the 1970s when there were a number of splits within the party, and a variety of new parties were formed, invariably with the word unionist somewhere in their title.

See also Act of Union, Home Rule, Loyalism, Nationalism, Partition, Republicanism, Stormont

United Irishmen

The Society of United Irishmen was founded in a tavern in Belfast in October 1791 by a small group of the city's leading merchants and intellectuals. Its policies were shaped by Theobald Wolfe Tone, a young Dublin barrister whose *Argument on Behalf of the Catholics of Ireland*, written a few months previously, had brought him to the attention of northern Presbyterian radicals. The founders of the United Irishmen were profoundly influenced by the ideals of liberty, equality and fraternity espoused during the French Revolution of two years earlier, and also by the publication of Thomas Paine's *The Rights of Man*, which sold some forty thousand copies in Ireland and was hailed by Tone as 'the Koran of Belfast'. In drawing up the 'Declaration and Resolutions of the United Irishmen of Belfast', Tone set out the aims of the society as the creation of 'a cordial union among all the people of Ireland' and the representation of 'Irishmen of every religious persuasion' in a parliament. These ideas found favour among Presbyterians, many of whom had wealth but no civil or political power, and also among Catholics, who were the most disadvantaged denomination in Ireland. In June 1795, Tone was joined by a small group of leading United Irishmen at McArt's Fort overlooking Belfast to make a solemn pledge 'never to desist in our efforts until we had subverted the authority of England over our country and asserted her independence'. This symbolic event is widely seen as the birth of Irish republicanism. Attempts to pursue their goal in the rebellion of 1798 failed and most of the leaders of the United Irishmen were executed, imprisoned or exiled. Tone committed suicide in jail rather than submit to execution by hanging.

See also Act of Union, Nationalism, Rebellion of 1798, Republicanism

U

Vikings

The Vikings were Scandinavian sea pirates whose first recorded attack on Ireland took place in AD 795. Monasteries and ecclesiastical settlements were their most frequent targets in the years that followed, not necessarily because the Vikings were anti-Christian, but at least partly because the religious communities were repositories of considerable wealth, livestock and food provisions. Gradually, sporadic raids gave way to attempts at colonisation, though domination and control proved more difficult in Ireland than in England because of the fragmented nature of Irish society and the number of regional overlords. Viking interest in Ireland waned temporarily, but by the middle of the tenth century there were a number of Viking settlements in Ireland.

Many had already converted to Christianity and were becoming assimilated into Irish society. They laid the basis for future towns – Dublin and Limerick in particular – struck their own coins and traded widely. The Battle of Clontarf in 1014, which has been widely portrayed as Brian Boru's greatest triumph over Viking invaders, was in reality a power struggle between would-be Irish kings, and Viking warriors actually fought on both sides. In the North, perhaps the most prominent reminder of the Viking legacy is in the names of two County Down sea loughs, Strangford and Carlingford.

151

Wakes

In Irish folklore there are many customs and rituals associated with death, and one of the best known is the wake, in which the deceased is given an often raucous send off by his family, friends and neighbours. Wakes were usually held over two nights, in the presence of the deceased, before the remains were removed to the church for the funeral. The body would often have been stretched out on the kitchen table and people would stay awake with it all night to ease the deceased's journey into the next world. Food and drink for the wake would generally have been supplied by the undertaker, and filled clay pipes were also provided for the guests. Games were a regular feature of wakes, and one of the most popular involved a group of men hiding a person's cap amongst themselves with the owner having to guess which one of them was holding it. A sense of jollity often prevailed at wakes because it was said that if you cried over the body of a dead person it brought them torment in the afterlife.

Whiskey

Distilled in Ireland as early as the sixth century AD, and possibly before, whiskey was given its most widely used name by twelfth-century Normans unable to pronounce the Irish *uisce beatha*, meaning 'water of life'. Made from barley, Irish whiskey differs from Scotch whisky not only in its spelling, but also because the Irish spirit is distilled three times, whereas in Scotland the boiling and condensing process is usually carried out only twice. Throughout the eighteenth century, Irish whiskey was considered to be far superior to Scotch and eight of the biggest

W

distilleries in the world were located in Ireland. However, a failure by many to adopt modern production methods, the introduction of prohibition in the United States (which decimated exports) and the superior business acumen of Scottish competitors led to a sharp decline in the number of Irish distilleries. In 1896 there were only twenty-eight left in Ireland out of a total of two thousand that had been in operation at the beginning of the century. Today only a handful remain, among them the world's oldest licensed distillery at Bushmills, County Antrim, which has been operating since 1608.

See also Poteen

Women's Institute

An organisation which aims to provide social contact for women in rural areas through the practice of country crafts, informal education and entertainment, and the encouragement of personal development. The first Women's Institute (WI) was founded in Canada in 1897 and the concept was taken up on the other side of the Atlantic shortly afterwards, leading to the formation of the National Federation of Women's Institutes in the United Kingdom in 1915. Members meet once a month and will often host guest speakers, hold quizzes and competitions, or go on outings. Often the monthly meeting will conclude with the singing of 'The Countrywoman's Song'. WIs in Northern Ireland hold an annual drama festival as well as area quizzes and bowls competitions.

Young Farmers' Clubs of Ulster

Despite the organisation's name, membership of the Young Farmers' Clubs of Ulster (YFCU) is not restricted to people with a farming background. It has been suggested that 'rural youth clubs' might be a more apt name for them, since membership is mostly regarded as an expression of rural identity and not all activities which the clubs undertake are connected with farming. The YFCU was founded in 1929 by William S. Armour, editor of the *Northern Whig* newspaper and son of J. B. Armour ('Armour of Ballymoney'), who was a champion of land reform and an advocate of home rule in the late nineteenth century. In August 1929, William Armour penned an article for the *Northern Whig* on the success of the Young Farmers movement in England and within two months the first Northern Ireland club was founded in Greyabbey, County Down. Young Farmers' Clubs are non-political and non-sectarian and are open to anyone between the ages of twelve and twenty-five. In addition to organising agricultural events, such as stock judging or farm visits, Young Farmers' Clubs also encourage cultural awareness and self-expression through public speaking, debating, crafts and drama.

Young Citizen Volunteers

A largely Belfast-based organisation formed in 1912 for young men aged between eighteen and thirty-five years. The aim of the Young Citizen Volunteers (YCVs) was to encourage 'responsible citizenship and municipal patriotism' through activities that were largely borrowed from the Scout and Boys' Brigade movements and then given more militaristic overtones. Although mostly made up of Protestants, the YCVs initially adopted a non-sectarian and non-political agenda, but this was gradually abandoned as the home rule crisis began to deepen and the YCVs became increasingly aligned with the Ulster Volunteer Force. In May 1914 the Young Citizen Volunteers became a battalion within the Belfast Regiment of the Ulster Volunteer Force and with the outbreak of World War I, became absorbed into the Fourteenth Battalion of the Royal Irish Rifles.

See also Battle of the Somme,
Boys' Brigade, Scout Movement

Y